Narnia in the Hands of Skeptics

By Reagan Schrock

NARNIA IN THE HANDS OF SKEPTICS

All Scripture quotes are taken, unless otherwise indicated, from the King James Bible.

Scripture references marked ESV are taken from the English Standard Version® (ESV®), copyright©, 2001. All rights reserved.

Printed in the United States of America

First edition

Table of Contents

Introduction

Few people can claim to have had more impact on Christian thinking in the last century as that of C. S. Lewis. Born in 1898, Lewis became convinced that there was no God after his mother died while he was still a boy. Through the influences of his colleagues at Oxford, Lewis became convinced that Christianity was true, and eventually came to believe in the redemption only offered through Christ. This occurred in 1931.

Soon after, Lewis began his writing career in his spare time between his duties at Oxford. Until his death in 1963, Lewis published dozens of books, volumes of essays, and delivered countless lectures. Today, the majority of his books and essays are still in print.

Perhaps the most impressive part of Lewis's literary career is the wide audiences he wrote for. While his field of study was primarily Medieval and Renaissance literature, he also authored books on apologetics, literary criticism, an autobiography, and Biblical studies, as well as several volumes of science fiction, myth, and children's literature.

His most popular and enduring achievement, however, is the seven-volume *The Chronicles of Narnia*. Written in the 1950s, this series has generated more discussion, controversy, and fans than nearly any other books in the genre of children's literature. An incredible 100 million copies of the seven volume series have been sold, as well as various theater and film adaptions. Countless books and articles have discussed nearly every conceivable topic in the series.

As often happens with popular media, much misunderstanding and misinterpretation of the Narnia series has occurred. Though the most common opinion is that this series is a masterpiece of children's literature and an enduring classic, others have questioned its teachings. On June, 2002, *The Guardian* printed an article titled "Narnia books attacked as racist and sexist." Phillip Pullman, who penned the popular His Dark Materials trilogy, accused Lewis's series as "propaganda" and said they were "monumentally disparaging of girls and women" as well as "blatantly racist." Children's literature scholar Peter Hunt shares similar theories against the Narnia books.[1]

Even more interesting is the fundamentalist Christians who claim that Lewis was a tool of the devil, and that Narnia is a tool for witchcraft. One article is titled "C. S. Lewis: The Devil's Wisest Fool."[2] A quick Google search will reveal dozens of other such articles.

When I first encountered the Chronicles of Narnia, I was amazed by some of the accusations against Lewis in general, and Narnia in particular. At first I was completely confused and decided to do my own research and see if what I was hearing had any merit. The result was several years of research reading countless of books and articles, plus spending untold hours in discussion with fans and critics alike. This book is the result.

My aim is not to give an exhaustive answer to all the accusations made against Lewis and the Narnia series. Rather, my intent is to provide an overview of what Lewis was trying to communicate. What were his goals and why did he write the series?

I do not claim to be an expert on C. S. Lewis nor his writings. Instead, I let the works of Lewis, as well as recognized authorities, be the final word as to what Lewis intended. With enough hard work, we can decipher what Lewis was trying to accomplish, and bring greater understanding to his life, time, and writings.

As this book will focus on just the seven volumes in the Chronicles of Narnia, it is assumed that the reader has a relatively good grasp of the story and plot laid out in the books. For example, I will not be explaining who certain characters are and which volumes they appear in, as well as other basic facts about the Narnian world. It is recommended that the reader consider rereading the series before beginning this book if they are not very familiar with each book and its characters and plot.

For the sake of brevity and conciseness, this book will use an abbreviation system when referencing any of the Narnia books. Each book will be referred to as follows:[3]

The Lion, the Witch, and the Wardrobe (LWW)

Prince Caspian (PC)

The Voyage of the Dawn Treader (VDT)

The Silver Chair (SC)

The Horse and His Boy (HHB)

The Magician's Nephew (MN)

The Last Battle (LB)

For page numbers, the mass-market paperback boxed set edition published by HarperCollins will be used.

It is my hope that in this book you will come to a greater understanding of who Lewis was and what his books were trying to communicate. However, no book can ever be perfect and this one is certainly no exception. Therefore, as I have likely made at least a few errors in the writing of this volume, I trust that the reader will continue to pursue the issues laid out in this book on their own. If this book does nothing else then spark the reason and imaginations of just a handful of readers, it will have been a success.

Reagan Schrock

April 12, 2015

Chapter One

C. S. Lewis' Purpose for Writing the Chronicles: Why Were They Penned?

Today there is an interesting philosophy spreading in Western thought. It is the idea of 'deconstructionism', a word coined by the French philosopher Jacques Derrida in his 1967 book *Of Grammatology*. His idea was that we should deconstruct literature to see what it means to the reader; it's kind of like tearing down a house to find out where the builder made a mistake. This philosophy states that it does not matter what the author actually wrote, but what it means to the reader and how it applies to them. It's kind of like saying 'the author must die so that the reader might live.' This explains why the modern paintings today are really just some paint slapped on canvas, with the intention that the viewer must interpret it and come to their own conclusions. This is simply deconstructionism at work. However, in reality, it doesn't matter what the words of the author mean to you, but the purpose and reason they are written, and the message they convey. In this chapter we will take a look at why the Narniad was actually written.

In this whole debate on C. S. Lewis and the Narnia series, perhaps the most important, yet most overlooked, part is this: what was his reason and inspiration behind this best-selling series? It does not matter what skeptics say about Lewis and why the Narnia books are wrong if they never consider his motives. This is by far the most critical part of this book, thus it will serve as the foundation for the following chapters.

The most important thing to keep in mind is what Lewis himself said about his works. Obviously, no one is more qualified to discuss the motive of a work other than the author himself, a point that Lewis refers to often: "Find out what the author wrote and what the hard words meant and what the allusions were to, and you have done far more for me than a hundred new interpretations or assessments could ever do."[4] And again:

> The first qualification for judging any piece of workmanship from a corkscrew to a cathedral is to know what it is- what it was intended to do and how it is meant to be used. After that has been discovered the temperance reformer may decide that the corkscrew was made for a bad purpose, and the communist may think the same about the cathedral. But such questions come later. The first thing is to understand the object before you: as long as you think the corkscrew was meant for opening tins or the cathedral for entertaining tourists you can say nothing to the purpose about them.[5]

In this chapter we will give the origin, background, and the reason behind the Chronicles of Narnia. However, so that this chapter will not just be my opinion weighted against the next person's idea, this chapter will refer to, and quote heavily from, recognized authorities on Narnia. But most importantly, it will be grounded in the other works of Lewis, both from his personal letters and his other fiction, as well as his autobiographical and theological books. First we will start with the origin of the Chronicles of Narnia. Where did the idea even come from, and does it affect the contents of the series?

Beginnings of Narnia: Origins and Inspiration

It is critical to understand that when Lewis wrote the first book in the Chronicles, he never intended to write more. After *Prince Caspian*, he was even surer that would be the last of Narnia. And by the time he penned *Voyage of the Dawn Treader*, he closed the book like the ending to a series, as can be seen with a critical reading of the final chapters of that volume. Fortunately for fans across the globe that was not to be, as the love for the story urged Lewis to add four more volumes. With this in mind, it becomes clear that once we find what inspired Lewis to write LWW we will be able to see where the idea for the rest of the series came from. It all starts in this book.

Where and when did Lewis come up with the idea for that first Narnia book? Until we answer this we can have little hope in find the true origin of the Chronicles.

It is impossible to point to one particular source of inspiration. Rather, there were many different factors that played roles in the development of this book.

> Lewis began the book [LWW] in 1939, perhaps as a consequence of having to entertain schoolgirls billeted at the Kilns in order to escape the London air raids.[6]

> The children at the center of events in LWW are wartime evacuees from the city and are billeted with Professor Digory Kirke. During the war Lewis, his brother, Mrs. Moore, and Maureen Moore lodged evacuees at different times in their Oxford house, The Kilns. The first two arrived in September 1940.[7]

Perhaps the best place where Lewis actually says what gave him the idea, and what he hoped to accomplish with it, is given in his short essay, "It All Began With a Picture..." It is given in its entirety below:

> The Editor has asked me to tell you how I came to write *The Lion, the Witch and the Wardrobe*. I will try, but you must not believe all that authors tell you about how they wrote their books. This is not because they mean to tell lies. It is because a man writing a story is too excited about the story itself to sit back and notice how he is doing it. In fact, that might stop the works; just as, if you start thinking about how you tie your tie, the next thing is that you find you can't tie it. And afterwards, when the story is finished, he has forgotten a good deal of what writing it was like.

> One thing I am sure of. All seven of my Narnia books, and my three science fiction books, began with seeing pictures in my

head. At first they were not a story, just pictures. The *Lion* all began with a picture of a Faun carrying an umbrella and parcels in a snowy wood. This picture had been in my head since I was about sixteen. Then one day, when I was about forty, I said to myself: 'Let's try to make a story about it.'

At first I had very little idea how the story would go. But then suddenly Aslan came bounding in. I think I had been having a good many dreams of lions about that time. Apart from that, I don't know where the Lion came from or why He came. But once He was there He pulled the whole story together, and soon He pulled the six other Narnian stories in after Him.

So you see that, in a sense, I know very little about how this story was born. That is, I don't know where the pictures came from. And I don't believe anyone knows exactly how he 'makes things up'. Making up is a very mysterious thing. When you 'have an idea' could you tell anyone exactly *how* you thought of it?[8]

From the information deduced above, we can confidently say that Lewis developed the idea for years before even starting. The origins of LWW are very straightforward in this regard: a simple picture on a wall, real life events, and numerous dreams sparked his active imagination. However, the big question is: was there any other inspiration in the back of his mind that affected the flow of the story? Many Christians hold to the idea that he was trying to teach certain Biblical concepts in the form of story. But was this actually the case?

The best way to see this topic clearly is to find what the author said about the work; a million theories can never replace the word of the creator of the work in question. So we start with something Lewis said in a letter dated December 24, 1959, sent to a schoolgirl named Sophia Storr in regards to the first book in the series:

> No, of course it was not unconscious [the Christian elements in the Chronicles]. So far as I can remember it was not at first intentional either. That is, when I started *The Lion, the Witch and the Wardrobe* I don't think I foresaw what Aslan was going to do and suffer. I think He just insisted on behaving in His own way. This of course I did understand and the whole series became Christian.[9]

This remark is quite telling. 'It was not at first intentional' is a bit interesting. Starting out Lewis did not have the idea of a Christian book. As we see above, he makes it clear that the whole series *became* Christian; it did not start out that way.

In one of his essays Lewis makes it clear as to the origin of LWW:

> Some people seem to think that I began by asking myself how I could say something about Christianity to children; then fixed on the fairy tale as an instrument; then collected information about child-psychology and decided what age group I'd write for; then drew up a list of basic Christian truths and hammered out 'allegories' to embody them. This is all pure moonshine. I couldn't write in that way at all. Everything began with images; a faun carrying an umbrella, a queen on a sledge, a magnificent lion. At first there wasn't even anything Christian about them;

that element pushed itself in of its own accord. It was part of the bubbling.[10]

Lewis could hardly make it more obvious that though there are Christian elements, they were not, at least at first, even on purpose. It appears that Lewis' mind was so conditioned to thinking and seeing this world through a Christian mindset that it spilled over into Narnia, without him having to give it conscious thought.

While perhaps on a popular level the layman may believe that Lewis made the Chronicles intentionally Christian, from the writings of Lewis himself we know this to not be true. It is also of interest to note that C. S. Lewis scholars would disagree with the popular beliefs surrounding the series. Perhaps the most qualified person to discuss the subject would be George Sayers, who personally knew Lewis and is one of his most widely acclaimed biographers. He says in his book:

> But the author almost certainly did not want his readers to notice the resemblance of the Narnia theology to the Christian story. His idea, as he once explained to me, was to make it easier for children to accept Christianity when they met it later in life. He hoped that they would be vaguely reminded of the somewhat similar stories that they had read and enjoyed years before. 'I am aiming at a sort of pre-baptism of the child's imagination.'
>
> Nevertheless, he did not, as is sometimes supposed, begin with a worked-out theological scheme in his head and write the stories to exemplify and inculcate it. The actual process was

less calculating; he wrote the stories because he enjoyed writing stories and always had.[11]

Lewis expounds on the above idea in one of his essays, making it very clear that the moral of the story works itself in of its own accord. He says of one of his earlier novels:

The story of this averted fall [in his adult novel, *Perelandra*] came in very conveniently. Of course it wouldn't have been that particular story if I wasn't interested in those particular ideas on other grounds. But that isn't what I started from. I've never started from a message or moral... The story itself should force its moral upon you. You find out what the moral is by writing the story."[12] In one review of *The Last Battle*, the reviewer comes to much of the same conclusion: "The child [reading the series] will not respond to these values [laid out in the Narniad] at once, though they will awaken in his memory when the time comes for full realization. Very possibly this latter service is the most startling one Lewis renders contemporary childhood... He touches the nerve of religious awe on almost every page. He evangelizes through the imagination.[13]

In one of his earlier novels (*Out of the Silent Planet* in 1938), Lewis used a similar technique. This book too he said he was writing for the sake of the story; the Christian values were secondary.

You will be both grieved and amused to learn that out of about sixty reviews, only two showed any knowledge that my idea of the fall of the Bent One was anything but a private invention of my own! But if only there were someone with a richer talent and more leisure, I believe this great ignorance might be a help to the evangelization of England: any amount of theology can now be smuggled into people's minds under cover of romance without their knowing it.[14]

Again, this wasn't the main focus for this novel nor the Narniad, but instead the Christian values worked their own way in simply because the personal beliefs of the author will shine through in his fiction, especially in the case of Lewis.

In a later section we will look closely at what Lewis believed about story and imagination, and how these can be a carrier of truth.

On Allegory

A very common idea about the Narniad is that these books are Christian allegories and that Lewis was trying to convey Biblical truths for children, deciding that story form would be best. As we saw in the above section, Lewis said this is not how the series was inspired. However, is it possible that Lewis, part way through, decided to put an allegory twist on the story?

First off, we must define allegory, particularly Lewis' definition of it. He said in chapter two of *The Allegory of Love*:

Allegory, in some sense, belongs not to medieval man but to man, or even to mind, in general. It is of the nature of thought and language to represent what is the immaterial in picturable terms. What is good of happy has always been high like the heavens and bright like the sun. Evil and misery were deep and dark from the first... This fundamental equivalence between the immaterial and the material may be used by the mind in two ways... On the one hand you can start with an immaterial fact, such as the passions which you actually experience, and can then invent *visibilia* [visible things] to express them. If you are hesitating between an angry retort and a soft answer, you can express your state of mind by inventing a person called *Ira* [Anger] with a torch and letting her contend with another invented person called *Patientia* [Patience]. This is allegory.[15]

Allegory is direct representation of an idea in an object. The best example would be the classic, *Pilgrim's Progress* by John Bunyan. In that volume, spiritual and nonmaterial concepts take on physical forms. Thus, the concept of despair comes in the form of a giant called Despair. This is allegory.

The question now is, does the Narniad fall into this category? The best way to find an answer is to go straight to what Lewis taught in his writings.

In his letters he discussed it with some of his readers. Lewis said this about the Narnia tales in a letter dated May 29, 1954:

You are mistaken when you think that everything in the books 'represents' something in this world. Things do that in *The Pilgrim's Progress* but I'm not writing in that way. I did not say to myself 'Let us represent Jesus as He really is in our world by a Lion in Narnia': I said 'Let us *suppose* that there were a land like Narnia and that the Son of God, as He became a Man in our world, became a Lion there, and then imagine what would have happened.' If you think about it, you will see that it is quite a different thing.[16]

The Chronicles were not intended to be direct representations of things in this world. It would be more accurate to say there are analogies and parallels, or *supposals* as Lewis called them.

In another letter, written December 29, 1959 to Mrs. Hook, Lewis further describes the concept of allegory:

By an allegory I mean a composition...in which immaterial realities are represented by feigned physical objects e.g.... in Bunyan [*The Pilgrim's Progress*] a giant represents Despair.

If Aslan represented the immaterial Deity in the same way in which Giant Despair represents Despair, he would be an allegorical figure. In reality however he is an invention giving an imaginary answer to the question, 'What might Christ become like if there really were a world like Narnia and He choose to be incarnate and die and rise again in *that* world as He actually has in ours?' This is not allegory at all. So [also] in [my book] *Perelandra*. This also works out a *supposition*.

Allegories and such supposals differ because they mix the real and the unreal in different ways. Bunyan's picture of Giant Despair does not start from supposal at all. It is not a supposition but a *fact* that despair can capture and imprison a human soul. What is unreal (fictional) is the giant, the castle, and the dungeon. The Incarnation of Christ in another world is mere supposal: but *granted* the supposition, He would really have been a physical object in that world as He was in Palestine and His death on the Stone Table would have been a physical event no less than his death on Calvary.[17]

Lewis could not be clearer that he did not intend to make these books into allegories. Rather, the idea was for them to be suppositions. There is a vast difference between the two and they must not be confused. In another letter to a school girl he talks about the same thing:

> ...it is not, as some people think, an *allegory*, that is, I don't say 'Let us represent Christ as Aslan.' I say, 'Supposing there was a world like Narnia, and supposing, like ours, it needed redemption, let us imagine what sort of Incarnation and Passion and Resurrection Christ would have there.' See?[18]

Despite these facts, many Christians have described the Chronicles as allegories. This is quite unfortunate as this is obviously not what they were meant to be. As Lewis says in the above example, Aslan is not a representation of Christ; he *is* Christ (in Narnia). The same applies to other Biblical themes that may come up in the series.

There is danger in trying to allegorize anything and

everything. Lewis referred to this several times:

...As we know, almost anything can be read into any book if you are determined enough. This will be especially impressed on anyone who has written fantastic fiction. He will find reviewers, both favourable and hostile, reading into his stories all manner of allegorical meanings which he never intended. (Some of the allegories thus imposed on my own books have been so ingenious and interesting that I often wish I had thought of them myself.) Apparently it is impossible for the wit of man to devise a narrative in which the sight of some other man cannot, and with some plausibility, find a hidden sense.[19]

And in another book:

...no story can be devised by the wit of man which cannot be interpreted allegorically by the wit of some other man....the mere fact that you *can* allegorize the work before you of itself no proof that it is allegory. Of course you can allegorize it. You can allegorize anything... I think we should here take a hint from the lawyers. A man is not tried at the assizes until there has been shown to be a prima-facie case against him. We ought not to proceed to allegorize any work until we have plainly set out the reasons for regarding it as an allegory at all.[20]

On Story

What is the role of story in the conveying of truth? Here we must look at what Lewis was hoping to accomplish through story, particularly children's stories. In reference to the use of story for children, he said:

> The child reader is neither to be patronized nor idolized: we talk to him as man to man.... We must of course try to do [children] no harm: we may, under Omnipotence, sometimes dare to hope that we may do them good. But only such good as involves treating them with respect.[21]

Perhaps one of the biggest mistakes we can make is in underestimating the power of story. For example, the extremely popular novel, *The Da Vinci Code* by Dan Brown, was released in 2003 and has since sold an astounding 80+ million copies. What is very interesting is the incredible impact of this story on the minds of its readers:

> A survey by Decima Research, Inc. showed that one out of three Canadians who have read the book now believes there are descendants of Jesus walking among us today. And according to pollster George Barna, 53 percent of Americans who've read the book said it had been helpful in their 'personal spiritual growth and understanding.'[22]

This isn't the only case. Phillip Pullman, author of the popular children's series His Dark Materials, said: "All stories teach, whether the storyteller intends them to or not. They teach the world we create. They teach the morality we live by. They teach it much more effectively than moral precepts and instructions."[23]

Popular Christian novelist Ted Dekker strongly believes that one of the best, if not the best, way to teach truth is through the power of story. He says of his novels:

> As a writer of fictional stories, I couch my convictions within the heart of full-length novels that characterize the struggle between good and evil. Not all stories attempt to dip into this struggle, but I find engaging the truth through a story tremendously useful and vital to my understanding of truth....We humans require story to understand truth.[24]

Perhaps the most under-estimated power in the world of learning is that of story; it is an excellent way to convey truth. Though some might disagree, we have clear proof of this in the Bible. Bible scholar Ray Vander Laan made the following points: "God delights in stories," and "God loves story" after noting that 80% of the Bible is in story form. In the Biblical times they tend to use story, word pictures, and dramatic action to convey truth.[25] Even Jesus taught difficult truths through parables, or stories. New Testament scholar N. T. Wright said of the early Christian church: "With the early Christians...stories were visibly and obviously an essential part of what they were and did."[26]

Lewis would have been well aware of these facts, as he had taught literature nearly all of his professional life. C. S. Lewis scholar Terry Glaspey points this out in his biography of Lewis:

Stories take us beyond ideas into the very experience of truth. After all, it was the promise of fulfilling the longing awakened by myths that had brought about Lewis' own conversion rather than careful logical analysis. Although he never ceased to believe in the power of the intellect to grasp the truth, it was in stories, Lewis found, that the truth of the Christian gospel could best be embodied and communicated.[27]

This does not mean, however, that Lewis was intentionally trying to 'preach' though story. As already discussed above, Lewis wrote the Chronicles because he loved a good story. The Christian themes worked their way in on their own. As it turns out it has proven extremely effective.

In the epilogue of *Out of the Silent Planet*, his first major novel, Lewis addresses why fiction was the best way to teach the truth in the book. Here he discusses the decision that he and 'Dr. Ransom' (the fictional hero in the story) came to:

It was Dr. Ransom who first suggested that our only chance was to publish in the form of *fiction* what would certainly not be listened to as fact. He even thought...that this might have the incidental advantage of reaching a wider public, and that, certainly, it would reach a great many people sooner [than nonfiction]... To my objection that if accepted as fiction it would for that very reason be regarded as false, he replied that there would be indications enough in the narrative for the few readers—the very few—who *at present* were prepared to go further into matter.[28]

Most significant in this quote is the line "this might have the incidental advantage of reaching a wider public, and that, certainly, it would reach a great many people sooner [than nonfiction]..." People are much more liking to listen to a story than bare facts. If Lewis had tried to teach the truth contained in the Chronicles through nonfiction instead of fiction, the impact would have been much less significant.

In a letter Lewis discussed this with one of his correspondents. The letter is summarized by Lewis scholar Kathryn Lindskoog:

On August 14, 1954, Lewis wrote to a Mrs. Donnelly telling her that he thought she had a mistaken idea of a Christian writer's duty. We are all obligated to avoid writing anything that will increase in our reader's lust, pride or ambition to outdo others; but we are only obligated to use the particular writing talent we have... Not all Christian writers are called to write specifically Christian works, and it is a mistake to tack on bits of Christianity [on the story]. A good story and a good meal are both innocent pleasures that don't need Scripture verses tucked in. The first job of a story is to be a good story; and if God wants the story to carry a Christian message, that will come in of its own accord. Lewis believed that some writing that is not obviously religious may do more good than some that is. Lewis concluded his advice... by saying that first we must fulfill whatever duties life imposes on us, and then we are to do whatever our natural talent points to. An honest work can be done to the glory of God, whether it is making stories, shoes, or rabbit hutches."[29]

The goal, in the end, is to bring God glory in everything we do. As Lewis points out, this was his intent from the beginning.

In fact, Lewis' own conversion was largely due to, or at least started with, a story from the great 19th century novelist, George MacDonald. He said in the introduction to his anthology of MacDonald: "What it actually did to me was to convert, even to baptize, (that was where the Death came in) my imagination. It did nothing to my intellect nor (at the time) to my conscience. Their turn came far later..."[30]

As Lewis points out in the above quote, sometimes the best way to convey truth to a person is in story form instead of straight, intellectual fact. Each person is different and in Lewis' case, the best way to start him on the path to Christianity was through story, which ultimately led to his conversion. Some people are beyond convincing through fact alone; sometimes to reach them we must go around the intellect by means of story form.

When he began the Chronicles of Narnia, Lewis had just written numerous apologetic works. He felt that it was time to communicate truth through a different medium, and had decided to do this through the use of "fiction and symbol."[31] This is precisely what he did, beginning with his science fiction trilogy (*Out of the Silent Planet, Perelandra,* and *That Hideous Strength*), which was published 1938-1945. There he had begun to explore themes that would later reveal themselves in the Chronicles. He makes himself abundantly clear in various letters:

Thanks for your letter. The day before I got a letter from someone else asking me if [my book, *Out of the Silent Planet*]... was a true story. It's not the first I've had. I'm beginning to think that some people (and if you don't look out I'll have to include you!) just don't understand what fiction is. When you say what is natural with the intention of making people believe it, that's lying. When you say it with no such intention, that's fiction. But it may be perfectly serious in the sense that people often express their deepest thoughts, speculations, desires etc. in a story.

As for 'writing stories about God,' it would be a rather tall order to have a story strictly about God… But to imagine what God might be supposed to have done in other worlds does not seem to be wrong: and a story is only imagining out loud.[32]

An even greater method is using not just story, but also imagination and fantasy within that story. This will be discussed in the next section.

Fantasy and Imagination

An important part of this discussion is Lewis' view and use of fantasy and imagination in his fiction. First of all, what did he believe about these concepts, and second, are they correct? And how did this affect his writing of the Narniad?

First, we must define fantasy. According to C. N. Manlove, lecturer in English literature at the University of Edinburgh, fantasy "…is that of a fiction evoking wonder and containing substantial and irreducible element of supernatural or impossible worlds, beings or objects."[33] In other words fantasy involves the supernatural, or things that are outside our world as we know it. By this definition, the Chronicles of Narnia are definitely fantasy;

it takes place in another world, in an unrealistic setting, and on a planet that doesn't exist.

So what was Lewis' point in writing a fantasy story? Why this particular form? And is fantasy healthy for the Christian, as it involves things that are most decidedly out of the realm of reality?

At first it is rather simple. Lewis loved a good fantasy story, and all his novels fall under the category of fantasy, or at least contain numerous fantastic elements. It makes sense that he would choose this form of story for the Narniad.

However, among more conservative Christians imagination and fantasy have been looked down on, sometimes even being considered dangerous to a person's spiritual health. As to be expected, in the Narnia debate one point quickly brought up is Lewis' use of fantasy and imagination. "Why read something that could never happen, in a world that doesn't exist, and about people who never lived, when you could be reading true stories about missionaries, or even novels that are at least based in this world, about real people?" is how the argument goes. Obviously, Lewis didn't see anything wrong with both reading and writing highly imaginative stories; in this section we will take a look at why, and if his reasons are legitimate.

Lewis wrote an autobiography about his childhood and the influence of books and imagination growing up. He makes an interesting point on imagination and fantasy:

> I had loved to read of strange sights and other worlds and unknown modes of being, but never with the slightest belief... It is a great mistake to suppose that children believe the things they

imagine; and I, long familiar with the whole imaginary world of Animal-Land and India (which I could not possibly believe in since I knew I was one of its creators) was as little likely as any child to make that mistake.[34]

Later he reaffirms this with:

One caution must here be repeated. I have been describing a life in which, plainly, imagination of one sort or another played the dominant part. Remember that it never involved the least grain of belief; I never mistook imagination for reality. About the Northerness no such question could arise: it was essentially a desire and implied the absence of its object. And Boxen we never could believe in, for we had made it. No novelist (in that sense) believes in his own characters.[35]

In fact, through fantasy we can get a better grasp of our own world. By reading about other worlds, we can come to appreciate ours more. His essay "On Three Ways of Writing for Children" he explains:

It [fairy tale] is accused of giving children a false impression of the world they live in. But I think no literature that children could read gives them a less of a false impression. I think what profess to be realistic stories for children are far more likely to deceive them. I never expected the real world to be like the fairy tales. I think that I did expect school to be like the school stories. The fantasies did not deceive me: the school stories did. All stories in which children have adventures and successes which are possible, in the sense that they do not break the laws of nature, but almost infinitely improbable, are in more danger than the fairy tales of raising false expectations.

Almost the same answer serves for the popular charge of escapism... Do fairy tales teach children to retreat into a world of wish-fulfillment—fantasy...—instead of facing the problems of the real world? .... Let us again lay the fairy tale side by side with the school story... There is no doubt that both arouse, and imaginatively satisfy, wishes. We long to go through the looking glass, to reach fairy land. We also long to be the immensely popular and successful schoolboy or schoolgirl, or the lucky boy or girl who discovers the spy's plot or rides the horse that none of the cowboys can manage. But the two longings are very different. The second, especially when directed on something as close as school life, is ravenous and deadly serious. Its fulfillment on the level of imagination is in very truth compensatory: we run to it from the disappointments and humiliations of the real world: it sends us back to the real world undivinely discontented. For it is all flattery to the ego. The pleasure consists in picturing oneself the object of admiration. The other longing, that of fairy land, is very different. In a sense a child does not long for fairy land as a boy longs to be the hero of the first eleven. Does anyone suppose that he really and prosaically longs for the dangers and discomforts of a fairy tale?—really wants dragons in contemporary England? It is not so. It would be much truer to say that fairy land arouses a longing for he knows not what. It stirs and troubles him (to his life-long enrichment) with the dim sense of something beyond his reach and, far from dulling or emptying the actual world, gives it a new dimension of depth. He does not despise real woods because he has read of enchanted woods: the reading makes all real woods a little enchanted. This is a special kind of longing. The boy reading the school story of the type I have in mind desires success and is unhappy (once the book is over) because he can't get it: the boy reading the fairy tale desires and is happy in the very fact of desiring. For his mind has not been concentrated on himself, as it often is in the more realistic story.[36]

Fantasy can be a great tool if we follow Lewis's advice. Simply take the story for what it is, all the while not confusing imagination and fantasy with reality. This is what separates the Narniad from many popular fantasy works today. For example, the popular Harry Potter series confuse reality with fiction. As one scholar stated: "Harry Potter is a fictional tale with a *nonfictional* backdrop..."[37] As a result, the line between what is real and what isn't becomes muddled. Lewis, on the other hand, penned a fantasy tale, set against a fictional backdrop. This makes for a great story that we can love, without confusing it with our own world.

However, this also means that though the story is completely removed from the present reality, it helps us to encourage a God given yearning for other worlds. Best-selling author Sarah Arthur notes that

> ...we hunger for other worlds. We long to go beyond the streets we know, beyond our familiar woods and fields, and into the land of Faerie; to Middle-earth, Narnia, or the Summerland....
>
> This longing isn't incidental. It's something we're born with. Most of us, if we're honest, sense with unease that this world is not all there is. At times we get inner hints and glimpse of *something* beyond what the eye can see. Eventually we begin to suspect that there is another Kingdom out there, perhaps closer

than we realize, possibly even just through that door.[38]

As Christians, we know that this is not the only world. There is another, spiritual world, one that Jesus called "the Kingdom of God." Though there is a thin veil between our world and it, sometimes we see the spiritual realm affect us, such as in the case of miracles.

There is a prevalent belief, especially among conservative circles, that imagination is unhealthy. One has to wonder what has caused this. We must now turn our attention to the issue of imagination.

Sadly, one reason for this wariness of the imagination comes from a misunderstanding. In the King James Version of the Bible, the word 'imagination' was slightly mistranslated. This has caused difficulties:

> *Imagination* seems to have become a suspicious word for the fundalit [fundamentalist/literalist]. One group of women wanted the middle-school textbooks banned because they were afraid that these school texts might 'stimulate the children's imaginations.'
>
> I was totally baffled until I realized that in the King James translation of Scripture the word *imagination* is not used as we use it; it does not mean opening ourselves to wonder; rather it is a negative word.
>
> Words change. Several translations now use the word *conceit* instead of *imagination*.

It is a mistake to assume that all words written in a translation several hundred years ago still mean the same thing today. What a sad loss it is to lose the current lovely meaning given to *imagination* and see it as something ugly! One small child at his uncle's burial watched the sky cloud over and rain beginning to fall, and said, 'God is crying.' How beautiful his imagination![39]

Here is an example of how the King James uses the word imagination. "And GOD saw that the wickedness of man was great in the earth, and that every imagination of the thoughts of his heart was only evil continually" (Genesis 6:5). However, the word that is translated imagination actually means something closer to "the intentions of man's heart." This is a much more correct rendering and is what newer translations now use.

Another example is in Luke 1:51: "He hath shewed strength with his arm; he hath scattered the proud in the imagination of their hearts." Again, imagination is the wrong choice. The Greek is closer to the word "understanding" and could be accurately translated as "the understanding of the heart."

Much of the problem that people have with the imagination is actually just a misinterpretation of what Scripture teaches.

There is an important distinction that needs to be made in this discussion, one that Lewis emphasized. In a recent Lewis biography, Alister McGrath points out that

Narnia is an *imaginative*, not an *imaginary*, world. Lewis was quite clear that a distinction had to be drawn between having no counterpart in reality. Lewis regards such an invented reality as opening the way to delusion. The "imaginary" is something that has been falsely imagined, having not counterpart in reality. Lewis regards such an invented reality as opening the way to delusion. The "imaginative" is something produced by the human mind as it tries to respond to something greater than itself, struggling to find images adequate to reality. The more imaginative a mythology, the greater its ability to "communicate more Reality to us." For Lewis, the imaginative is to be seen as a legitimate and positive use of the human imagination, challenging the limits of reason and opening the door to a deeper apprehension of reality.[40]

Once this distinction is made, much of the confusion on this matter is removed. We can begin to understand that imagination, as Lewis was referring to, can be a very powerful tool for the Christian. If we can capture the imagination for the glory of God, consider the good we could accomplish.

This is what Lewis was trying to do with the Narnia books. As we saw in the previous section, Lewis believed in the baptized imagination. He explains how this happened through the writings of George MacDonald: "What it [one of MacDonald's books] actually did to me was to convert, even to baptize... my imagination. It did nothing to my intellect nor (at the time) to my conscience. Their turn came far later..."[41] Lewis was trying to convert his reader's imagination and in the process, bring them one step closer to experience God. As we can see, this is what eventually converted him to Christianity. It was not the intellect (though that played a major role), but actually the imagination.

Respected theologian Oswald Chambers points out in his

famous devotional, *My Utmost for His Highest*, while commenting on Isaiah 40:26:

> The people of God in Isaiah's time had starved their imagination by looking on the face of idols. But Isaiah made them look up at the heavens; that is, he made them begin to use their imagination correctly. If we are the children of God, we have a tremendous treasure in nature and will realize that it is holy and sacred. We will see God reaching out to is in every wind that blows, every sunrise and sunset… if we will only begin to use our starved imagination to visualize it.

> One of the reasons for our sense of futility in prayer is that we have lost our power to visualize. We can no longer even imagine putting ourselves deliberately before God. The power of imagination is what God gives a saint so that he can go beyond himself and be firmly placed into relationships he never before experienced.[42]

One of Lewis's good friends, Dorothy Sayers, said that "The Christian faith is the most exciting drama that ever staggered the imagination of man."[43] The Church is in great danger of forgetting the awesomeness of what God has done for us. People like Lewis were attempting to "baptize" our imaginations so that we could come to better grips with what God has done and who he is.

In this section we have attempted to point out how imagination can be a very powerful tool of the building of God's Kingdom; yet this would not be complete without noting the dangers as well. Sayers sums it as such: "The language of the imagination can never be inert; as with every other living force, you must learn to handle it or it will handle you. 'The question is,' said Humpty Dumpty, 'which is to be the master—that's all.'"[44] Though the imagination is of great importance and is the center of creativity, it must be noted that it can take a person where they should not go. We must learn to approach fantasy and imaginative works with the correct perspective, having our feet firmly planted in reality before we attempt to navigate the nebulous world of fantasy. We must understand the uses of this powerful tool, and keep in mind that it can, and very often is, used to teach philosophies and worldviews that are not in alignment with God's character.

Conclusions

Lewis, quite clearly, was not trying to write an allegory. The best judge of what he was attempting to portray is what he himself said about the series, and we see clearly from his writings that he was simply writing a good story. The Christian element came afterward, and when it did Lewis decided to use story and imagination as a tool to stimulate the minds of his readers in themes that are ultimately rooted in the Bible.

To close off the chapter it is fitting to quote one of Lewis's essays at length. This was written in a book of essays on literature, and was in response why he wrote the Narnia series.

On that side (as Author) I wrote fairy tales because the Fairy Tale seemed the ideal Form for the stuff I had to say.

Then of course the Man in me began to have his turn. I thought I saw how stories of this kind could steal past a certain inhibition which had paralyzed much of my own religion in childhood. Why did one find it so hard to feel as one was told one ought to feel about God or about the sufferings of Christ? I thought the chief reason was that one was told one ought to. An obligation to feel can freeze feelings. And reverence itself did harm. The whole subject was associated with lowered voices; almost as if it were something medical. But supposing that by casting all these things into an imaginary world, stripping them of their stained-glass and Sunday school associations, one could make them for the first time appear in their real potency? Could one not thus steal past those watchful dragons? I thought one could.[45]

Chapter Two

On Magic

Perhaps the most common reason that numerous people have an issue with the Chronicles is because of the heavy use of magic throughout. In this chapter we will cover the objections and some possible responses.

It is quite obvious that in every book there is a heavy reliance on magic. Indeed, every trip into Narnia happens through magic. As can be clearly seen in the Bible, magic is a serious sin, and is equated with Satanism and idolatry. How can we reconcile this with what we see in Lewis's writings?

Definitions

First, it should be clarified what is meant by the word

'magic.' In the case of the critics, they are generally referring to that of occult magic, which has its roots in spiritual darkness and is undoubtedly evil. Scripture often addresses this. In the 21st century we are encountering this form of dark supernatural forces in day to day life. Many popular teen novels as well as TV shows portray this magic in graphic detail.

But how did C. S. Lewis view the use of the magic? Though he never addressed this topic in full, there are many places scattered about in various writings where he does mention magic and its definitions.

He defines magic as "how to subdue reality to the wishes of men."[46] Unlike miracles, magic is a formula for obtaining what our wishes are. Both are supernatural, but God's way of miracles is outside of human control.[47]

But there's more. Magic, in the end, destroys the person who wields it. In the same volume he writes

> ...the magician's bargain: give our soul, get power in return. But once our souls, that is, ourselves, have been given up, the power thus conferred will not belong to us. We shall in fact be the slaves and puppets to that to which we have given our souls.[48]

Just a year earlier Lewis had published his famous *Screwtape Letters*. In the preface to that volume he carries his theology of magic further still, equating the practice of magic with Satanism:

There are two equal and opposite errors into which our race can fall about the devils. One is to disbelieve in their existence. The other is to believe, and to feel an excessive and unhealthy interest in them. They themselves are equally pleased by both errors and hail a materialist or a magician with the same delight.[49]

Magic, in the view of Lewis, was not just practicing the works of Satan, but entailed literally bartering the soul away. Obviously, this is something Lewis viewed as extremely evil.

Interestingly, Lewis struggled with the desire of the occult before coming a Christian. He writes in his autobiography *Surprised by Joy* that

…there burst upon me the idea that there might be real marvels all about us, that the visible world might only be a curtain to conceal huge realms uncharted by my very simple theology. And that started in me something with which, on and off, I have had plenty of trouble since—the desire for preternatural, simply as such, the passion for the Occult. Not everyone has this disease; those who have will know what I mean. I once tried to describe it in a novel [That Hideous Strength]. It is a spiritual lust; and like the lust of the body it has the fatal power of making everything else in the world seem uninteresting while it lasts. It is probably this passion, more even than the desire for power, which makes magicians.[50]

The Nature of the Spiritual and Physical in Our World

A major theme throughout almost all of Lewis' works

is that of the relationship between the physical world and the spiritual. Within his view, these two elements were much related; the barrier between the physical and spiritual was thin. When this barrier was crossed, miracles occurred.

Throughout his life, Lewis devoted entire books to this fascinating relationship, most notably in his theological book *Miracles* (1947) and short novel *The Great Divorce* (1946).

Yet he did not hold to the view that the spiritual realm was less "real" then this world. In his famous sermon "Transposition" Lewis defines clearly what he means:

> It is the present life which is diminution, the symbol, the etiolated, (as it were) 'vegetarian' substitute. If flesh and blood cannot inherit the Kingdom, that is not because they are too solid, too gross, too distinct, too 'illustrious with being.' They are too flimsy, too transitory, too phantasmal.[51]

The spiritual world is not only a reality, but is much more "real" than this world; it is the ultimate reality. In the end, Heaven is the only thing that is truly and literally real. Earth and our universe is only a shadow and glimpse of the great spiritual reality that God has created.

Throughout our lives we do see glimpses of this Other World in miracles, the Bible, sometimes in creation itself. But on the whole, we don't see this spiritual universe on anything that could be called a frequent basis.

But what if there were a world where the spiritual and

physical mingled?

The Magic of Narnia

In the Narnia stories, this is exactly what we see. But in that world, the supernatural comes in the form of magic. As we saw above, Lewis was not in favor of magic as we define it. What if the supernatural was taken out of its earthly context? Would it not look very similar to the magic of fairy tales?

Just as in our world, where there are 'battle lines' between the good and evil powers, so too in Narnia there is two sides to this supernatural ('magical') element.

Though this sounds like a good theory, it means nothing if we cannot show that this is what Lewis intended.

Tolkien, who was friends with Lewis for many years, discussed something very similar with his fantasy writings:

> Tolkien thoroughly disliked having to use the word *magic*, but was forced to do so because he could find no other word closer to the meaning he intended.[52]

The meaning intended was the presence, in a very real way, of the supernatural in a fantasy world. This is virtually identical to the problem Lewis encountered with the Narnia stories. In an article discussing the issue of magic, the same conclusion is come to:

We can affirm that the Bible condemns sorcery and black magic in our world because they *do exist* as tools of a *real* devil on a *real* Planet Earth. But we can also know—and help our children know if they ever doubt—that Narnia is in a different category. It's real only like Mickey Mouse is real. For this same reason, Narnian magic, which is made-up, is different from earthly black magic, which is often real.[53]

This is something that we noted above in defining magic. Lewis strongly stated that *earthly* magic is real and deadly; it is something that will destroy us.

But later in life Lewis sheds more light on what he means by the term 'magic' when not referring to the earthly magic of Satanism. In his last book (*Letters to Malcolm*), he discusses the 'magic' of what Christians refer to as the Lord's Supper:

I do not know and can't imagine what the disciples understood Our Lord to mean when, His body still unbroken and His blood, unshed, He handed them the bread and wine, saying *they* were His body and blood....for me the something which hold together and 'informs' all the objects, words, and actions of this rite is unknown and unimaginable... Yet I find no difficulty in believing that the veil between the worlds, so thin and permeable to divine operation. Here a hand from the hidden country touches not only my soul but my body. Here the prig, the don, the modern in me have no privilege over the savage or the child. Here is big medicine and strong magic... When I say 'magic' I am not thinking of the paltry and pathetic techniques by which fools attempt and quacks pretend to control nature. I mean rather what is suggested by fairy-tale sentences like 'This is a magic flower, and if you carry it the seven gates will open to you of their own accord,' or 'This is a magic cave and those who enter it will renew their youth.' I should define magic in this sense as 'objective efficacy which cannot be further analysed.' ...there must always remain the utterly 'brute' fact...that a universe— or, rather, *this* universe with its determinate character—exists; as 'magical' as the magic flower in the fairy-tale. Now the value, for me, of the magical element in Christianity is this. It is a permanent witness that the heavenly realm, certainly no less than the natural universe and perhaps very much more, is a realm of objective facts—hard, determinate facts, not to be constructed *a priori*, and not to be dissolved into maxims, ideals, values, and the like... Enlightened people want to get rid of this magical element in favour of what they call the spiritual element. But the spiritual, conceived as something thus antithetical to 'magical,' seems to become merely the psychological or ethical. And neither that by itself, nor the magical by itself, is a religion. I am not going to lay down rules as to the share...which the magical should have in anyone's religious life. Individual differences may be permissible. What I insist on is that it can never be reduced to zero. If it is, what remains is only morality, or culture, or philosophy.[54]

Once again we see that Lewis is contrasting the two worlds of the spiritual and physical realms. What Lewis is referring to here, as he notes, is a different kind of 'magic.' This is the supernatural element of Christianity, the mystical nature of God and salvation. Without this element, he argues, we cease to properly understand what Christianity really is.

What We Find in the Books Themselves

This discussion would never be complete without examining what is actually contained within the books themselves. All the theories mean very little if we do not see anything to prove them within the Narniad.

The first thing to note is that good magic in Narnia, without exception, either finds its origins in, or is directly associated with Aslan, which is clearly a Narnian figure of Christ.[55] This clearly parallels with the miracles that Jesus Himself performed. There are only two possible exception to this: Cornelius in PC, and Coriakin in VDT.[56]

In the case of Cornelius, it is somewhat undetermined if he even is a 'good' character. Though he means well and plays a large role in the return of the Old Narnians, there are various points in his magic and beliefs that make us question the authenticity of his character. His lack of faith in Aslan comes out in various places; when Nikabrick attempts treachery, Cornelius is notably silence in the defense of Aslan. While Trufilhunter stands for Aslan and the power of Susan's horn, Cornelius states he is "disappointed in the results of the operation" (PC, page 174). It seems that in some ways Cornelius is a 'gray' character; he means well, but sometimes we have reason to wonder how loyal to Aslan he really is. It is important to remember that his only source of information about Narnia, Aslan, and the four Kings and Queens was from legend and stories passed down for over a thousand years. It seems that his belief in reason and science is stronger than in Aslan.

A very similar thing could be said about Coriakin in VDT. There are hints that all is not well with his character. We first note this when Lucy begins reading from the magician's book. When she attempts one of the spells, that of eavesdropping on her friends, she finds out just how harmful it can be. The spell Lucy does not attempt (to make her beautiful beyond all mortals) would clearly have been a very harmful spell, and in fact she does not say it because Aslan himself appears on the page to warn her against it (VDT, page 165). After Lucy makes the Dufflepuds visible again, Coriakin himself addresses the issue of magic. After Aslan asks if he is tired of looking after the Dufflepuds, Coriakin responds: "Sometimes, perhaps, I am a little impatient, waiting for the day when they can be governed by wisdom instead of this rough magic" (page 174). We get the impression that his magic is more of a necessary evil, and inferior to simple wisdom.

Further into the tale, on Ramandu's Island, we learn that indeed Coriakin was not, at least in the past, a good character at all. Previously he had been a star but was sent to earth in judgment, until one day he could be worthy of being a star again (VDT, page 226).

A second thing to note is that in the entire series, there is no good magic that occurs outside of the Narnian context. In every case of magic that is not Narnian in origin ('other world'), it is clearly shown to be wrong.[57] There are only two clear instances of magic outside of Narnia, in MN and SC. In the first case, Uncle Andrew attempts to be a magician. However, as the book develops, we can see that this is not a healthy exercise. In the end, evil is brought into Narnia and Aslan forbids further use of the magic rings. It is also clear that Andrew is not a character that is to be looked up to in any way. Never again in the series do we see magic that is non-Narnian used to get to Narnia. This brings us to the example in SC.

In the first chapter, Eustace tells Jill of Narnia, and in an attempt to get away from bullies, they decide to try and get to Narnia again. Jill suggests that "...we might draw a circle on the ground—and write in queer letters in it—and stand inside it—and recite charms and spells?" Clearly this refers to some sort of magical spell to grant one's wish. But note that Eustace replies "...I've an idea that all those circles and things are rather rot. I don't think he'd like them. It would look as if we thought we could make him do things. But really, we can only ask him" (SC, page 7). The children decide to call on Aslan instead.

What Jill suggests (likely out of ignorance) is not something Aslan would deem right. Instead, quite unexpectedly, they gain entrance to Narnia by simply asking. This reflects, in some ways, the difference between prayer and magic. Both are supernatural; however, magic is a formula to get your wish. Prayer is calling on a higher Power (in this case, Aslan), who will not always grant our every whim.[58] Sometimes people try and take matters into their own hands instead of depending on God. When we try to manipulate the elements to get our wishes instead of going through God, we are, in a sense, attempting magic.

Narnian Magic Versus 21st Century Children's Literature

In the 21st century, a much different approach to magic is playing a predominate role in children's literature. This could be clearly noted perhaps first in J. R. Rowling's series, *Harry Potter*. Some have made the mistake of comparing this series with the works of Lewis and Tolkien; there is, however, a significant difference in how these authors approached the issues of the supernatural and magic. In the Rowling stories, the context is completely different.

The origin of the supernatural element in this particular series, and others like it, is far from clear. Both the 'good' and 'evil' characters use very similar forms of the supernatural to try and conquer each other.

Often times the magical element is within the context of real-world life. For example, Harry Potter lives in a literal, factual place in England. Richard Abanes points out "Harry Potter is a fictional tale with a *nonfictional* backdrop..."[59] Because of this, Abanes concludes "The distance between Rowling's fantasy world and real-world occultism is just too short." The lines between what is Rowling invention and what is real life are hard to distinguish.

This has created an entirely different genre then the one instigated by Lewis and Tolkien in the last century. While their work and Rowling's are both fantasy, the latter has taken the storyline out of the fantasy world and brought it into everyday life. The tales of Narnia are clearly in an unrealistic setting. And rightly so, as the story was written for its own sake as simply a good story. What has happened over the last several decades is the explosion of literature involving a very real backdrop. The differences between the 'good' and 'evil' supernatural elements (a vital part of any work of fantasy) are becoming less distinct.

It is also worth noting the time era that the Narnia books were written. In that day, magic and fairy tales were becoming less of a staple in the normal reading diet of children. In previous generations, being raised on fairy tales was normal. In 20th century England, however, it was becoming more popular to focus on reality and what we can see and test scientifically.[60] The Narnia series, as well as most of his other fiction, was an attempt to reverse this movement. Little would Lewis realize that he had, with the help of Tolkien's *Lord of the Rings*, practically recreated the genre of fantasy and brought exposure to the fantastic story into everyday life. As the genre grew, elements emerged that Lewis could never have imagined. Today, the vast majority of the fantasy literature being produced is shallow and weak, far from the moving work of Lewis and the Inklings. With this new wave of fantasy literature has also come a massive increase in the occult. Now, the works of fantasy and fairy tale have been degraded to the level of occult repackaged into an entertainment framework.

As we've seen, this is an area where Lewis stands out. His supernatural elements (magic) are in a different world entirely; whenever they occur in this world they are negative.

Conclusion

From the works of Lewis himself, we are able to compile a framework for which Lewis put the power we call 'magic.' He clearly disapproved of earthly magic, believing it would lead to the destruction of the person who tried to harness it. As we can see, the magic of Narnia falls under an entirely different category, and was Lewis's way of explaining the presence of the supernatural in an other worldly context.

We can see from the Narniad itself that magic in its earthly context is never endorsed, and is even strongly discouraged in several cases. In the end, the great concern expressed against the use of magic in this series comes down to a misunderstanding of the terms involved. Once we understand what Lewis meant and was trying to communicate, the difficulty disappears. This also helps us to discern what fantasy works are healthy today, and helps point out the difference between what Lewis wrote and those of more modern authors such as Rowling.

Chapter Three

Theological Parallels in Narnia

Throughout this book so far, we have covered numerous objections people put forward against the Chronicles of Narnia. One of these is that these books, if they are really Christian, should contain plenty of obvious connections to the Bible. If Lewis was a Christian, surely he would have done this. This chapter will do is go book by book through the series, and take a look at some of the many parallels to Scripture enclosed in their pages. Note that this list is by no means exhaustive in its coverage. To do so would probably fill a small book of its own.

In this chapter we will only look at the ones where it is obvious that Lewis was trying to mix in themes from the Bible. If you look hard enough, you could find many examples that could possibly be taken from Scripture. However, in some cases this is just simple coincidence.

The Lion the Witch and the Wardrobe

In his first book he wrote in the series, published in 1950, Lewis weaves an interesting combination between two worlds as well as the natural and supernatural. The LWW contains some of the best lessons to be learned out of the entire series.

It is interesting to note that the entire book is built around a strong theme of the redemption of a country and its people. It is also a clear analogy of a person's heart. Though this doesn't make it an allegory, it seems that Lewis did want to get across a strong message of salvation through this book. When the children first enter Narnia, they find it a frozen, lifeless world, held in the grip of an evil Witch. The whole country is without color, unchanging from its state for a hundred years.

But that all changes with the coming of Aslan. Narnia is made new, color and life return, and the Witch's rein starts to crumble. Just as Christ brought life to this world and destroyed Satan's grip on it, Aslan does the same in LWW. Wrong is made right, life and hope are returned to the Narnians and evil conquered. It seems that Lewis simply took an unseen reality in this world (that of evil, Satan, and spiritual lifelessness) and put it into the physical realm in Narnia. The world's foremost authority on the Narniad notes this:

> It is significant that Lewis wrote the Chronicles, particularly *The Lion, the Witch and the Wardrobe* and *Magician's Nephew*, at the same time he was writing his autobiography, *Surprised by Joy*. Just as Lewis's first chronicle tells how Aslan brings spring to the land of Narnia after a seemingly endless winter, *Surprised by Joy*

describes how God restored Lewis's feelings and faith, both of which had been frozen after the death of his mother, Florence Lewis.[61]

An interesting element Lewis creates in this tale is the fact of the various prophecies concerning the coming of Aslan. One hardly has to point out that this is very similar to the numerous foretellings of the coming of Christ. In both cases, accurate predictions are made; each foretell the salvation of an oppressed people; and peace can only return when the Christ, or Aslan, comes, not before.

Another part where Lewis seems to have been influenced by the Bible and seems to have gotten straight from Scripture is the small Narnian poem that Mr. Beaver tells the four children:

Wrong will be made right, when Aslan comes in sight,

At the sound of his roar, sorrows will be no more,

When he bares his teeth, winter meets its death,

And when he shakes his mane, we shall have

spring again (LWW, page 85).

Wrong will be made right: this phrase looks as if it was taken from Matthew 12:20: "A bruised reed shall he not break, and smoking flax shall he not quench, till he send forth judgment unto victory." *"At the sound of his roar"*: this is almost a direct quote from Hosea 11:10: "They shall walk after the LORD: he shall roar like a lion: when he shall roar, then the children shall tremble..." *"Sorrows will be no more"*: here Lewis appears to be referring to Isaiah 65:19, which says: "And I will rejoice in Jerusalem, and joy in my people: and the voice of weeping shall be no more heard in her, nor the voice of crying." In fact, this entire poem carries the same kind of hopeful longing that the Jews had for the coming Messiah, for their salvation. In the Bible they often are crying out for God to save them, and it appears that Lewis puts this same longing inside Narnians.

Even in the character of Father Christmas there seems to be a hint of Biblical inspiration. Says Narnia scholar Christin Ditchfield: "Father Christmas brings each of the children gifts. These gifts are 'tools not toys'—tools that will help them fulfill their calling and face the challenges ahead. According to the Scriptures, Jesus sent the Holy Spirit to give believers spiritual gifts 'to each one, just as he determines' (1 Cor. 12:11...)."[62]

Perhaps the most important character transformation is Edmund. To the watchful reader, it is clear that Edmund is a form of the fallen disciple Judas, who betrayed Jesus. In Narnia, Edmund betrayed his family, the entire world of Narnia, and most of all, Aslan Himself. In our world, Judas also betrayed his "family" (the other disciples), betrayed his world by selling his Creator to be killed. The only major difference between Judas and Edmund is how the story ends. In the case of Judas, he realizes the gravity of what he has done (as does Edmund) and commits suicide. Edmund, on the other hand, accepts Aslan's forgiveness and goes on to become an important character in later Narnia stories.

Here Lewis is exploring something he did in various other works of fiction: delving into the great questions of "What if?" For example, an earlier novel he touches on what if Adam and Eve's Fall had been adverted? In that book, he creates another world where Satan is trying to make its inhabitants fall into the grip of Evil.[63] In another work of fiction, Lewis attempts to picture what Heaven would look like to sinners who were given a second chance to convert after death.[64] In LWW, he considers what might have happened if Judas would have seen his mistake and become saved. What might have happened is the story of Edmund.

After the Narnians rescue Edmund from the White Witch, Aslan brings him to his brother and two sisters. He says: "'Here is your brother,' he [Aslan] said, 'and- there is no need to talk to him about what is past'" (LWW, page 153). This is a good analogy of how God forgives and forgets the sins of those who are truly repentant of them. This statement seems to mirror the verse of Isaiah 65:16: "The former troubles are forgotten, and…they are hid from mine eyes."

When the White Witch meets with Aslan, she tells of the "Deep Magic" and says: "…every traitor belongs to me as my lawful prey and that for every treachery I have a right to a kill" (page 155). This echoes the oft quoted verse, Romans 6:23: "For the wages of sin is death…" All sinners are enemies of God and, in a sense, are traitors, therefore under Satan's control. The same truth apparently applies in Narnia.

Not only that, the White Witch also states that the price of Narnia's freedom must be paid in blood (LWW, page 156). This too applies to our world; the cost of redeeming mankind had to be paid in blood through the cross (Hebrews 9:22).

Just before Aslan meets the Witch on the night before his

death, Lucy and Susan follow him through the wood. Here we see Aslan, for one of the only times in the Chronicles, actually sorrowful, reluctant, and perhaps even fearful. When Aslan discovers them, we see how deeply sad and lonely he is, knowing what is about to happen to him. This seems to be patterned after the Gospels' accounts of Jesus in the garden of Gethsemane, the day before He was crucified. At that time, too, Christ was alone, fearful, and greatly longing to not have to go through the events of the following day. As Lewis is shown to have attempted to do with the character of Aslan (showing what Christ might have been like in a different world), he masterfully gives a glimpse of what it was like for Jesus, yet in a way young children can understand. Aslan says "I shall be glad of the company tonight" (LWW, page 164). This is an echo of what Christ tells His disciples in Gethsemane: "...tarry ye here, and watch with me" (Matthew 26:38). And again, when Aslan says that "I am sad and lonely" (LWW, page 164) it reflects the part of the same verse that says "My soul is exceeding sorrowful, even unto death..."

Lewis did very clearly model the Stone Table sacrifice around the crucifixion. As with Jesus, the White Witch and her followers laugh, mock, and jeer at Aslan (LWW, pages 165-170). Lewis could not make himself more clear when he says, about Aslan, that "...had the Lion chosen, one of those paws could have been the death of them all [the Witch's followers]. But he made no noise..." (LWW, page 166). As we know, Christ went to the Cross of His own will and could have destroyed all of His enemies with the lift of a finger. But He "...opened not his mouth" (Isaiah 53:7, ESV), just as Aslan was silent and did not fight back. Lewis gives us an accurate description of the sacrifice of Jesus. Randy Alcorn, who speaks highly of C. S. Lewis, says this about the sacrifice of

Aslan:

> Children can learn a great deal about Jesus by watching
> Aslan on the stone table, knowing he could have killed his
> mocking enemies with a single word, but instead allowing
> himself to be bound, laying down his life for Edmund.[65]

When Aslan rises from the dead, it is important to note that the "Stone Table [was] broken into two pieces by a great crack that ran down it from end to end..." (LWW, page 177). What would give Lewis the idea to put this in his book? A very probable answer is found in Matthew 27:51: "And, behold, the veil of the temple was rent in twain from the top to the bottom; and the earth did quake, and the rocks rent." Both the temple curtain and the Stone Table were torn completely in half.

After Aslan's resurrection, which is also influenced by the Gospels' account of Jesus rising from the dead, he tells Lucy and Susan that "...though the Witch knew the Deep Magic, there is a magic deeper still which she does not know. Her knowledge goes all to the dawn of time. But if she could have looked a little further back, into the stillness and the darkness before Time dawned, she would have read a different incarnation. She would have known that when a willing victim who had committed no treachery was killed in a traitor's stead, the Table would crack and Death itself would start working backward" (LWW, page 178-179). This is incredibly similar to what the Apostle Paul writes about the death of Christ: "But we impart a secret and hidden wisdom of God, which God decreed before the ages for our glory. None of the rulers of this age understood this, for if they had, they would not have crucified the Lord of glory" (I Corinthians 2:7-8, ESV).

At first, Susan's response to seeing Aslan again is identical to how the disciples reacted when they first saw Jesus alive. Susan thought that perhaps he was a ghost, reflecting what the disciples said: "...they were terrified... and supposed that they had seen a spirit" (Luke 24:37). Then Aslan does something significant. Throughout the Chronicles, he breathes on people which gives them strength and courage to face difficulties. This is the first time it happens, which he does to convince Susan that he is not a ghost (LWW, page 178). This bears remarkable resemblance to John 20:22, where Jesus, after He is raised, "he breathed on them and saith unto them, Receive ye the Holy Ghost."

After the battle, Aslan feeds the entire army of Narnians in an obvious miracle. The narrator of our story describes the scene: "How Aslan provided food for them all I don't know; but somehow or other they found themselves all sitting down on the grass to a fine high tea at about eight o'clock" (LWW, page 198). One hardly has to point out this is an echo of Jesus feeding the five thousand, recorded in Matthew 14.

Though Lewis was not trying to write a Christian allegory, it is very clear that he weaves many Biblical themes and ideas into the first Narnia book. He wasn't attempting to preach to his readers, but much theological data can be found in the pages he wrote.

Prince Caspian

In the second Narnia book to be published, Lewis does not weave in nearly so many direct reflections from Scripture.

However, the theme of the book, taken as a whole, does seem to be inspired by Aslan (Christ) and the saving of a lost, disillusioned country.

When the Pevensie children left Narnia, after they had reigned there for fifteen years, they were in what was known as the golden years of Narnia. After their disappearance, Narnia was never the same. When Prince Caspian is born 2275 years later, many Narnians had forgotten all about Aslan, the four kings and queens, and no longer ruled their own country. They were the 'People in Hiding.' With the coming of Aslan, this all changes. Peace is restored, the Telmarines are defeated, and finally the old Narnia is back. For the first time in centuries the trees come alive and the woods people are awakened. This is very like the message of LWW, in that Aslan is once again the salvation of a country that cannot be freed by any other. Is this not what God does to individuals, peoples groups, and even countries that are willing to accept His help? The well-known verse of 2 Chronicles 7:14 is finally what the Narnians did: they choose to seek the help of Aslan by blowing Susan's horn.

As for as direct connections to the Bible, this book has very few. An obvious one where Lewis basically quotes the Bible is in chapter 12, when several of the Narnians are discussing their next move. So far the war had been going badly for them and they were wondering if the horn had even worked at all. The dwarf Nikabrick does not believe help will come, but the badger Trufflehunter says to him, "The help will come. It may be even now at the door" (page 174). This is almost identical to Mark 13:29, which says "So ye in like manner, when ye shall see these things come to pass, know that it is nigh, *even* at the doors." In PC this verse is literal because in that story, help *was* just on the other side of the door.

When Lucy meets Aslan for the first time, he tells her a difficult truth, that her obedience must not be determined by the response of others, even family: "If they will not [follow], then you at least must follow me alone" (page 151). This is a clear reflection of one of the sayings of Jesus when teaching about the cost of following Him, even when others do not: "He that loveth father or mother more than me is not worthy of me: and he that loveth son or daughter more than me is not worthy of me" (Matthew 10:37).

After Aslan awakens the Old Narnia again, Aslan, Lucy, Susan, and some of the others come upon on old woman who is about to die (as the reader finds out later, it was actually Prince Caspian's nurse who was banished because she told him stories about the Old Narnia). Aslan heals her, and then it seems as if Lewis puts into this story something that was inspired by Jesus' first miracle, the turning of water to the richest wine (John 2:7-9). A cup of water was drawn for the old woman, but when it was given to her, "…it now was not water but the richest wine, red as red-currant jelly…" (page 217).

As mentioned above, throughout the Narniad Aslan breathes on people to rid them of their fears and renew their courage. We again see this near the end of the book. The first Telmarine who decides to go through the door Aslan creates (to return to earth) is given a special blessing by Aslan, who then breathes on him (page 234). The allusion to John 20:22, where Jesus' breath is used as a carrier of the Holy Ghost, is quite clear.

The Voyage of the Dawn Treader

Unlike the two before it, VDT is more of an adventure novel. Because of this, the message of good conquering evil does not come out as strong as in the previous volumes. Even so, Lewis masterfully wove various biblical themes into this volume.

After Eustace is un-dragoned, he meets Edmund in the forest. When his tale is told, Edmund says that it must have been Aslan that restored Eustace into a boy again. Eustace asks 'Do you know him?' 'Well—he knows me,' said Edmund" (page 117). Since God is all-knowing, obviously He knows us quite well; perhaps even better than we know ourselves. Here Lewis is conveying a great truth that the Apostle Paul writes about: "For now we see in a mirror dimly, but then face to face. Now I know in part; then I shall know fully, even as I have been fully known" (I Corinthians 13:12 ESV). Later in his life Lewis explored this fact in his last book, *Letters to Malcolm* (published posthumously). In that book he says "We are always completely, and therefore equally, known to God. That is our destiny whether we like it or not....this knowledge never varies..."[66]

Note also that Eustace could not fix the problem himself; only Aslan could. We cannot rid ourselves of the 'dragonish' nature we have; only God can do this. After he is changed into a boy, Eustace explains that "...he [Aslan] caught hold of me...and threw me into the water. It smarted like anything but only for a moment. After that it became perfectly delicious and as soon as I started swimming and splashing I found that all the pain had gone from my arm. And then I saw why. I'd become a boy again" (page 116).

Here Lewis seems to be making an interesting point. As part of Eustace being un-dragoned, he was submerged in a mountain pool. It wasn't this act that removed his dragon self; only Aslan could do that. But notice that this change was not quite complete, or perhaps finalized, until Aslan put Eustace in the pool. If Lewis is implying baptism in this part of his book, which definitely makes sense, then he does it very accurately. Here the baptism was just the finishing touches on Eustace's salvation. It was not essential. This is exactly how baptism works in the Bible; salvation is first, and then, if possible, baptism. Lewis gives us, in the telling of the transformation of Eustace, a true-to-life example of salvation; in this case, the evil inside a person is manifest on the outside as well.

Also note the order Lewis does this. First Aslan must remove Eustace's dragon self, thereby implying salvation; then Aslan submerges him in the pool; thus the baptism. First comes repentance and salvation, and only after that is baptism, according to the instruction of Scripture.

One last thing to note with the transformation of Eustace. Recall that Eustace could not change himself, no matter how hard he tried. Only Aslan could do that. I believe Lewis was here making a point that often comes up in his nonfiction works: that of Christianity not being about simple self-improvement, but about God completely transforming us into something new and different. He writes in *Mere Christianity*: "It may be hard for an egg to turn into a bird; it would a jolly sight harder for it to learn to fly while remaining an egg."[67]

Of all the Chronicles, this book is perhaps the only one that has a direct reference to prayer. This is during the episode of the Dark Island. It seems as if the ship is lost in the blackness, and the crew has little hope of survival. Lucy "leant her head on the edge of the fighting-top and whispered, 'Aslan, Aslan, if ever you loved us at all, send us help now.' The darkness did not grow any less, but she began to feel a little—a very, very little—better" (page 200). After this, an albatross appears in a beam of light, who is really Aslan in different form. He comes and breaths on her, which as mentioned above, is a symbol of Christ giving the Holy Ghost to His disciples in John 20:22. After this the albatross leads the *Dawn Treader* out of the Dark Island and disappears. This likely is alluding to our calls of distress to God when we are in our own form of the Dark Island, which God promises He will hear.

Later on in the story, when the Narnians reach Ramandu's Island, Lucy sees a very interesting sight: "But Lucy, looking out from between the wings of the birds that covered her, saw one bird fly to the Old Man [Ramandu] with something in its beak that looked like a little fruit, unless it was a live coal, which it might have been, for it was too bright to look at. And the bird laid it in the Old Man's mouth" (page 223). This is very similar to Isaiah 6:6-7: "Then one of the seraphim flew to me, having in his hand a burning coal that he had taken with tongs from the altar. And he touched my mouth and said: 'Behold, this has touched your lips; your guilt is taken away, and your sin atoned for.'"

When the children meet Aslan at the end of the world, he makes an interesting point when he tells them about getting to Aslan's Country from their world: "…I will not tell you how long or short the way will be; only that it lies across a river. But do not fear that, for I am the great Bridge Builder" (page 269). This description of Aslan being the way to his Country is a clear parallel to what we know of Christ. He is the one way to Heaven. When Thomas asked Jesus how he could travel to where Jesus was going, the Messiah replied that He was "the way, and the truth, and the life. No one comes to the Father except through me" (John 14:6, ESV).

At the end of this story, Lewis gives perhaps the clearest hint in the Narniad that he was influenced by the Bible. When the two Pevensies and Eustace come to the End of the World, they meet a Lamb who offers them breakfast of fish roasted over a fire. At first they don't notice it is Aslan, but he then reveals himself to them as the Lion. Lewis apparently obtained this idea straight from the Gospel of John. Near the end of that book, John describes a scene after the Resurrection. Several of the apostles had go ne fishing, but caught nothing. As they returned to shore, they saw a man standing there but could not tell it was Jesus (John 21:4). After this, He gave them breakfast of fish roasted over a fire, and said the exact words Aslan used: "Come and have breakfast" (verse 12, ESV). This is almost identical to how Lewis portrays the same scene in Narnia. It is abundantly clear where he got his inspiration for this part of the story.

The Silver Chair

In this book, the fourth to be published, Lewis himself wrote that the Biblical theme had been somewhat lowered, saying vaguely that "[The theme of] *The Silver Chair* [was] the continued war against the powers of darkness."[68] However, there are still a distinct number of references throughout to the Bible.

One point that Lewis seemed to be stressing through its pages is that of the Word of God. A Lewis scholar has this to say about the book:

...the central theological concept for the plot of [The Silver]

Chair is the emphasis on learning and remembering Scripture. This takes the form of Aslan's giving Jill four 'Signs' to remember. When she has them learned, Aslan tells her to 'remember, remember, remember the Signs. Say them to yourself when you wake in the morning and when you lie down at night.' The Signs clearly parallel the laws give to Moses on Mount Sinai.... Aslan's instructions on how to remember parallel the instructions about the laws given to the Israelites: 'And these words, which I command thee this day, shall be in thine heart...when thou liest down, and when thou risest up' (Deut. 6:6, 7b).[69]

Almost right away, Lewis points us back to the Bible. In chapter two, Jill is desperate for a drink of water. She meets a Lion (Aslan) in the forest, and he tells her, "If you're thirsty, you may drink" (page 20). This points us back to John chapter four, when Jesus offers the Samaritan woman His living water (see John 4:10, 13-15).

Jill is hesitant to drink from the stream because she is afraid that Aslan will try to attack (after all, he is a Lion). She says to him, "'I suppose I must go and look for another stream then.' 'There is no other stream,' said the Lion" (page 21).

Here it seems quite likely that Lewis is referring the reader back to John 7:37-38: "Jesus stood and cried, saying, If any man thirst, let him come unto me, and drink." The New Testament makes it clear that Christ is the only source of living water. In a sense, there really is no other stream with which we can truly satisfy our thirst.

Shortly after that, Jill confesses to Aslan that the reason Eustace fell off the cliff was because she was showing off her lack of fear of heights. When Aslan hears this, he replies "'That is a very good answer, Human Child. Do so no more'" (page 22). After this, Aslan is less stern with her and doesn't mention the incident again. This parallels quite well with Jesus and the woman caught in adultery. The Bible records His response: "'Woman, where are those thine accusers? Hath no man condemned thee?' She said, 'No man, Lord.' And Jesus said unto her 'Neither do I condemn thee: go, and sin no more'" (John 8:10). It is a distinct possibility that Lewis was, subtly, directing his audience back to this story in the Bible.

Then Alan makes a very interesting statement. He tells Jill that he has called her and Eustace out of their world for a special task. At first Jill is confused, believing that they had called on Aslan instead, and not the other way around. To this he replies: "You would not have called to me unless I had been calling to you" (page 23). This hints at the teachings of Jesus where God is the one calling us, not the other way around. Jesus says in one of His sermons that "No one can come to me unless the Father who sent me draws him" (John 6:44, ESV). The same truth in this verse is also referred to in Revelation 17:14.

It is not until much later in the story that we encounter any other clear references to Biblical passages in this Chronicle. An interesting statement is made by Puddleglum that seems to be pointing us back to the New Testament. When our heroes are trapped in the giants' castle, Puddleglum reminds the two children that Aslan's instructions "always work; there are no exceptions" (page 124). This reminds us of God's words in Isaiah 55:11: "...my word...will not return to me empty, but it shall accomplish that which I purpose, and shall succeed in the thing for which I sent it"

(ESV).

In chapter thirteen, when the heroes of the story are seemingly trapped in the Underworld, Prince Rilian says, "'... Aslan will be our good lord, whether he means us to live or die. All's one, for that'" (page 200). This compares well with what Paul wrote to the Romans: "For if we live, we live to the Lord, and if we die, we die to the Lord. So then, whether we live or whether we die, we are the Lord's. For to this end Christ died and lived again, that he might be" (Romans 14:8, ESV).

When Caspian dies, it seems that Lewis draws much from how Christ responded to the death of his friend, Lazarus. Similarities abound: Caspian is a very good friend of Aslan; Lazarus is also the friend of Jesus. After Caspian's death, Aslan wept (page 251), as Christ did for Lazarus. And in the end, both Caspian and Lazarus are raised to life again by Jesus and the Narnian edition of Him, Aslan.

Towards the end of the tale, in chapter sixteen, Eustace and Jill meet Aslan again, shortly after King Caspian dies. The only thing Jill can think about is how she forced Eustace off the cliff, and forgot the signs. She wants to tell Aslan how sorry she is, and he tells her, "Think of that no more. I will not always be scolding" (page 250). This is a beautiful and accurate portrayal of Christ. When we are most repentant of our failings is when He is the most merciful. Here Psalms 103:9 (ESV) fits perfectly: "He will not always chide, nor will he keep his anger forever."

At the end of SC, Lewis draws from Scripture perhaps the most clearly of the entire Narniad outside of the ending of VDT. In the final chapter, just before Aslan sends the children back to their own world, King Caspian, who has died and is in Aslan's Country with them, asked if he could see just a glimpse of our world. Aslan gives Caspian permission to return to earth for a short time with Eustace and Jill. Lewis wrote the tale thus:

'Are coming with us, Aslan?' said Jill.

'They shall see only my back,' said Aslan.

"He led them rapidly through the wood, and before they had gone many paces, the wall of Experiment House appeared before them. Then Aslan roared so that the sun shook in the sky and thirty feet of the wall fell down before them.... Aslan turned to Jill and Eustace and breathed upon them and touched their foreheads with his tongue. Then he lay down amid the gap he had made in the wall and turned his golden back to England, and his lordly face toward his own lands (page 255).

Those even vaguely familiar with the Bible will immediately notice the connection here. Aslan is Christ (and God the Creator) in that world. This world is only able to see his back, and even this is almost too much for the people who see him. This is clearly borrowed from the story of Moses, the only human being recorded to have seen God. Like in SC, Moses saw only the back of God, through a crack in the rock: "Then I will take away my hand, and you shall see my back, but my face shall not be seen" (Exodus 33:23 ESV).

The Horse and His Boy

HHB is perhaps the most interesting of the entire Chronicles, though with the least direct parallels to the Bible. The role of Aslan in this volume is fascinating and clearly points back to the Trinity.

Author Christin Ditchfield points out that the overarching theme of the book is clearly Biblical in this regard: "Many spiritual treasures can be found in HHB. But there is one powerful, overriding theme throughout the story, that of divine providence: God at work behind the scenes."[70] More than any of the other books in the series, HBB reveals the character of Aslan and leaves no doubt that Lewis is talking about Christ.

Aslan plays a predominate role in four of the fifteen chapters, though we aren't told this until Shasta meets him in the mountains of Archenland. The most obvious thing we note is that, as Ditchfield states above, Aslan's providence shines through as a central theme. This is first seen in chapter two, when Aslan is directly responsible for the four travelers meeting each other (pages 27-30). Later on, Aslan defends Shasta by the tombs from the desert jackals (pages 94-95).

Towards the end of the book, Aslan comes into the story even more. In chapter ten, Aslan is responsible for causing the horses to run just fast enough to warn the Archenlanders in time (page 151). He even directly reveals himself to Aravis, Bree, and Hwin, showing them that he is a real being (page 215). This encounter directly reflects that of Christ with doubting Thomas (John 20:26-31). Thomas was not convinced that Jesus was really risen from the dead and actually in the flesh. In the same way, Bree believed Aslan was not a real lion. Aslan shows himself to Bree, telling him to "draw near. Touch me. Smell me. Here are my paws, here is my tail, these are my whiskers. I am a true Beast" (page 215). Though Aslan is a supernatural being, he is also a physical Lion. This is the great mystery of the incarnation, where Christ was God, and yet at the same time a physical Man.

Aslan also clearly distinguishes the difference between fate and providence in his conversation with Shasta. Shasta says that "I am the unluckiest person in the whole world!" and proceeds to tell Aslan his story. To which Aslan replies "I do not call you unfortunate" and begins to explain to Shasta that it was not fate that caused his misfortunes, but rather that it was guided by Aslan himself from the very start (pages 174-175).

During Shasta's meeting with Aslan on the mountain, we catch one of the few glimpses of the Trinity within the Chronicles. Though we do get glimpses of the Trinity in some of the other books, this is probably the clearest incident.

'Who are you?' asked Shasta.

'Myself,' said the Voice, very deep and low so that the earth shook: and again 'Myself,' loud and clear and gay: and then the third time 'Myself,' whispered so softly you could hardly hear it, and yet it seemed to come from all round you as if the leaves rustled with it (page 176).

This encounter reflects most clearly the Trinity, in that Aslan reveals himself in three different ways: power, clear, and soft. These can easily be compared to the basic characteristics of the Trinity: God the Father is seen as all-powerful, Jesus Christ is direct and clear in his teaching, and the Holy Spirit is thought of as the still, small voice of God.

At the same time, this also bears many similarities to when God revealed himself to Moses. In that incident, when Moses asked who he was, God simply replied with 'I AM' (Exodus 3:14), much like Aslan replying 'Myself.' Lewis could have hardly been clearer in making this encounter a reflection of Moses' meeting with God in Exodus.

Throughout the entire work, there is a strong feel of the love of Aslan for the Calormenes. Strangely, numerous critics have taken some of the components in this story to try and prove that Lewis was indicating racism. This we will ignore for the time being, and will answer in chapter four.

Lewis was deeply concerned about the unsaved people around him, a fact clearly seen in many of his books written for non-Christians. We can't help but wonder that perhaps this is why he includes the conversion of Aravis from Tash to Aslan, the only one of its kind in the series.[71] This is likely the 'hidden' theme of this book, and something Lewis indicates in a letter several years after the book's publication.[72]

Of all the books in the Narniad, HBB contains some of the best character transformation. Ones that most clearly stand out are that of Shasta, Aravis, and Bree. Again, in each of these cases Lewis sticks closely to his 'theme' of salvation for those who have never heard of Aslan (Aravis and the Calormenes), or have distorted views of who he really is (Bree and Shasta, for example). Perhaps one worth noting the most is that of Aravis.

One of the main thrusts of Lewis's writings, both fiction and nonfiction, was to bring people to God and Christianity. In fact, many of his religious works were aimed at a non-Christian audience.[73] In HHB, Lewis weaves a fascinating tale of the redemption of those lost to false religions. Aravis is the most obvious example, though Shasta, Bree, and Hwin are as well.

She starts her life as a Calormen princess. But the Calormen culture is bound by the worship of Tash, and is a cruel place with a slave trade and forced marriages.[74] Wanting to break free from this hopeless cycle, she runs away to Narnia. Along the way, Aravis and her horse, Hwin, meet Shasta and Bree, who then all travel to freedom together. Each character, in their own way, goes through a journey in search of truth and the real Aslan. For example, Bree believes in Aslan, but does not think he is a Lion. Hwin doesn't really say what she believes, but when confronted with the real Lion himself, she is the first to accept. Shasta is not sure how he feels about the subject, but in the end completes his journey by meeting the Lion. However, Aravis is the most interesting.

As a Calormen, the impression is strong that she does not believe in Aslan to begin with, but rather follows Tash (at least outwardly). When she decides to run away to Narnia, Aravis leaves all of this behind in hopes for something better. This book could well be described as the journey of Aravis to find true religion and freedom. This is what is found in Aslan. Towards the end of the story, she meets him face to face and in the end completely rejects her previous life in Calormen, becoming a true Narnian at last. Aslan blesses this and she later became one of the greatest queens of Archenland.

This is a vivid picture of our journey to find true freedom and the real Christ in this world. Conversion and repentance is more of a journey than anything; this is something John Bunyan points out well in *The Pilgrim's Progress*. It also a major theme in the other writings of C. S. Lewis, particularly his allegory *The Pilgrim's Regress* (written shortly after he became a Christian and in many ways autobiographical) and his autobiography, *Surprised by Joy*, which tells the story of his personal journey to belief in Christ. Coming to Christ never happens in an instant, but rather is the end result of our journey through life, looking for true joy, peace and freedom. This, Lewis is telling us, is only found in Christ (Aslan in that world).

The first time a direct quote from Scripture occurs in the first chapter, when Bree is describing the land of Narnia to Shasta. He says: "An hour's life there is better than a thousand years in Calormen" (HHB, page 10). This rings similar to Psalms 84:10, which tells us: "For a day in your [God's] courts is better than a thousand elsewhere" (ESV).

The next time we see another reference is not until chapter fourteen. Here we find Aravis, Hwin, and Bree in the house of the hermit, when Bree is telling them what he thinks Aslan is like (arguing that his is not a real Lion at all). In the height of irony, Aslan suddenly arrives, to the shock of them all, as a real Lion. Hwin, despite her obvious fear of lions, is the first of the group to surrender to, and trust in, him. Aslan's response is kind and seems to echo quite distinctly one of the teachings of Christ. "Dearest daughter... I knew you would not be long in coming to me. Joy shall be yours" (HHB, page 215). One cannot help but notice first of all Aslan's willing acceptance of her; but more importantly, his final phrase, *"Joy shall be yours."* This seems to reflect a verse in the Gospel of Matthew (25:21 ESV): "His master said to him, 'Well done, good and faithful servant. You have been faithful over a little; I will set you over much. Enter into the joy of your master.'" This is what the lord in Jesus' parable tells the faithful servant.

It is of interest to note how both Aslan and the lord in the parable (representing Christ) responded to the situation in similar ways. Though it may be a stretch to claim that Lewis borrowed from this passage when writing the HHB, it is a fine example of how Christian themes naturally found their way into his works of fiction.

Another time in this volume where it appears that the Bible influenced Lewis's thinking is in the last chapter. Here we encounter the somewhat humorous story of Rabadash the Ridiculous, a Calormen prince who is a little too proud for his own good.

After the battle with Rabadash and his Calormen army, he is captured and held in the castle of King Lune. The Narnians give him a fair trial, but he turns down their attempts to deal honestly with him.

And then, Aslan appears among them. He warns Rabadash to stop fighting and make peace with Narnia. Instead, Rabadash curses them, saying Tash will destroy them. Though Aslan offers freedom to him, Rabadash rejects this and instead calls Aslan a demon, refusing to repent. For his wickedness, Aslan turns him into a donkey, saying that Rabadash could become a man again only if he stood before all Calormen at the Autumn Feast, and there the shape of the donkey would leave him.

This sounds very much like the story of King

Nebuchadnezzar in Daniel 4. It can easily be imagined that Lewis had this in mind when he formed this part of the story. Nebuchadnezzar, for his evil actions, is made as one of the beasts in the field, at least mentally. Scripture tells: "and he was driven from men, and did eat grass as oxen..." (Daniel 4:33). The parallels of this compared to Rabadash can clearly be seen, with some variation. In fact, Lewis twists it just enough to make it different, but still retains the idea of its origin. For example, in the Bible Nebuchadnezzar stays in human form, but wild in mind like an animal. In HHB, Rabadash turns into the form of a beast, and instead keeps the mind of a human.

It also is worth pointing out that both Nebuchadnezzar and Rabadash were punished for the same reason: pride. The Bible is very clear: "The king spake, and said, 'Is not this great Babylon, that I have built for the house of the kingdom by the might of my power, and for the honour of my majesty?'" (Daniel 4:30) In the last verse of the chapter, the king makes it clear this was the result of his pride: "...those that walk in pride he is able to abase" (Daniel 4:37).

The Magician's Nephew

In this volume, Lewis gives an interesting spin on Genesis, but in a different world. What would have the Creation story looked like in a different world? What would have been the same? And what would have been different? Opposite of what some skeptics of Lewis's writings say, Lewis did not believe in evolution, progressive creation, or the gap theory and millions of years.[75]

In fact, most of the Biblical allusions in this book happen

when Aslan creates Narnia (chapters 8 through 11). Earlier, Lewis again warns against pride, much as he did in HHB. It was by the pride of Digory that brought Jadis into Narnia; this helps the reader realize the high price of not having humility. The stakes are high, not just in that world but also in this one.

Until we come to chapter eight, there is not much to cover for this study. But when we do, things get very interesting. With the creation of Narnia, Lewis weaves in obvious components from the Book of Genesis.

The main characters find themselves brought into a different world when they try to rid our world of Jadis. Lewis describes it as "…uncommonly like Nothing. There were no stars. It was so dark that they couldn't see one another at all and it made no difference where you kept your eyes shut or open. The air was cold and dry and there was no wind" (page 114). This is very clearly parallel to Genesis 1:2: "And the earth was without form and void; and darkness was upon the face of the deep." Lewis from the very start of the creation of Narnia borrows heavily from Scripture.

Lewis once said, in so many words, that what is considered myth in one world may be fact in another one. This is exactly what Lewis does in the first part of the Narnian creation.[76] On pages 116 and 117 of MN, we read:

> Then two wonders happened at the same moment. One was that the voice was suddenly joined by other voices; more voices than you could possibly count. They were in harmony with it, but far higher up the scale: cold, tingling, slivery voices. The second wonder was the blackness overhead, all at once, was blazing

with stars. One moment there was nothing but darkness; next moment, a thousand, thousand points of light leaped out... The new stars and the new voices began at exactly the same time. If you had seen and heard it, as Digory did, you would have felt quite certain that it was the stars themselves which were singing, and that it was the First Voice, the deep one, which had made them appear and made them sing.

I believe it to be very reasonable to suggest that here Lewis was taking what is fiction in our world and making it fact in another. Likely inspiration would be from the book of Job, chapter 38, verse 7. Speaking of the creation, God tells Job about "When the morning stars sang together..." Though this likely is a non-literal verse, Lewis, in another world, takes the same idea and makes it reality in Narnia.

On page 133, Lewis describes how the animals were created out of the ground by Aslan. This is identical to Genesis 1:24: "...God said, Let the earth bring forth the living creature after his kind..." In this world, as at the beginning of Narnia, the creatures were literally created out of the earth. It seems that Lewis is exploring what it may have been like if you could have been there to see it.

When Aslan is talking to Digory about how he had brought Jadis into Narnia, Aslan tells him, "As Adam's race has done the harm, Adam's race shall heal it" (page 162). This clearly echoes the teaching of the Bible; Paul writes that "For...by man came death..." (I Corinthians 15:21). And in the second part of Aslan's statement ("Adam's race shall heal it"), Lewis borrows the fact that the Christ was one of us, from the line of Adam and completely human, yet without sin. Again Paul brings this out in I Corinthians 15, where he calls Jesus the "last Adam." As in Narnia, this world was redeemed by a son of Adam, known as Jesus the Christ.

When Aslan is giving instruction to the first king and queen of Narnia, Lewis pulls an almost direct quote from the Bible. Aslan tells them to "be just and merciful and brave. The blessing is upon you" (page 204). This is very similar to a verse in the Book of Micah: "what doth the LORD require of thee, but to do justly, and to love mercy, and to walk humbly with thy God?" (Micah 6:8)

After Aslan makes Frank and his wife the first king and queen of Narnia, he instructs them: "You shall rule and name all these creatures..." (page 164). This obviously pulls from Genesis and the instruction God give to Adam and Eve at the beginning to care for the animals He created: "And let them [humans] have dominion over the fish of the sea and over the birds of the heavens and over the livestock and over all the earth and over every creeping thing that creeps on the earth." (Genesis 1:26 ESV) In the second chapter of Genesis God also tells Adam to name the creatures, just like the quote by Aslan above: "[God] brought [the creatures] unto Adam to see what he would call them: and whatsoever Adam called every living creature, that was the name...." (Genesis 2:19)

In chapter fourteen, Aslan says to Uncle Andrew: "Oh Adam's sons, how cleverly you defend yourselves against all that might be good" (page 203). This follows the lament of Christ over Jerusalem in Matthew 23:27: "O Jerusalem, Jerusalem...! How often would I have gathered your children together as a hen gathers her brood under her wings, and you would not!"

In the new world Narnia, the first temptation was to eat an apple from the tree in the center of the garden. Jadis (the

White Witch) promised that it was "the apple of youth, the apple of life….Eat it, Boy…and you and I will both live forever" (page 192). This reminds one of the temptation of Eve in Genesis 3. There Satan convinced her to eat fruit from a tree in the Garden of Eden, promising that "you will not die." (Genesis 3:4) As in LWW, however, Lewis again explores another "what if?" question. What if Eve would not have fallen to the Serpent's lies? Digory is his way of exploring this issue, much as Lewis did in his previous novel *Perelandra*.

After Digory completes the mission Aslan gave him, Aslan says to him: "Well done" (page 197). This is an exact quote from Jesus' parable of the good steward. When the servant successfully finishes the task required of him, his master, who represents God, tells him: "Well done, thou good and faithful servant…" (Matthew 25:21).

The Last Battle

LB concludes the Chronicles of Narnia, telling how that world came to an end. Many consider this the best book of the Narniad; it is worth noting that it won the 1956 Carnegie Award.[77]

Lewis himself said in a letter that "*The Last Battle*: the coming of the Antichrist (the Ape). [And] the end of the world and the Last Judgment."[78] Many of the elements match the events predicted to come to pass in our world. Through this piece of fiction we can get a better feel for what is ahead for us on earth. From the very start Lewis brings into Narnia some of the events that will signal the end of our world.

In the first chapter, as the elements leading to the end of the Narnia are beginning, an earthquake occurs when Shift doubts Aslan's involvement in their world (page 13). This goes closely with the warnings Jesus gives concerning the end of time: "For nation shall rise against nation, and kingdom against kingdom: and there shall be earthquakes in divers places, and there shall be famines and troubles: these *are* the beginnings of sorrows" (Mark 13:8). Scripture, particularly Revelation, speaks often of the fact (Revelation 6:12; 8:5; 11:13; 11:19; and 16:18).

In the next chapter, reference is made to signs in the sky, such as the stars. Roonwit, a centaur prophet, explains: "...the sky would have foretold [Aslan's coming]" (page 19). This echoes Amos 3:7: "For the Lord God does nothing without revealing his secret to his servants the prophets" (ESV).

In the same conversation Roonwit says to the king: "Never in all my days have I seen such terrible things written in the skies as there have been nightly since this year began" (page 18). From the signs he foretells great disaster for Narnia. Old Testament prophecy speaks often of the signs in the heavens, particularly Joel: "The earth shall quake before them; the heavens shall tremble: the sun and the moon shall be dark, and the stars shall withdraw their shining" (2:10); "And I will shew wonders in the heavens and in the earth, blood, and fire, and pillars of smoke" (2:30).[79]

One of the main points that Shift the Ape makes in an attempt to deceive them is trying to convince the Narnians that "Tash is Aslan: Aslan is Tash" (page 40). Quite likely the Antichrist of this world will try the same thing, hoping to confuse who Jesus is with the forces of darkness. Through all of history people have made every effort to tell us that Christ was not who He said and was really quite like the leaders of other religions. Isaiah refers to this very thing in the fifth chapter of his book, verse 20: "Woe to those who call evil good and good evil, who put darkness for light and light for darkness, who put bitter for sweet and sweet for bitter!" (ESV)

In this same chapter, King Tirian tries to expose the falsity of this teaching. He attempts to ask them "how the terrible god Tash who fed on the blood of his people could possibly be the same as the good Lion by whose blood all Narnia was saved" (page 42). Notice carefully the statement "the good Lion by whose blood all Narnia was saved."[80] This clearly is very much in line with a familiar part of one of Paul's letters: "In him we have redemption through his blood, the forgiveness of our trespasses, according to the riches of his grace" (Ephesians 1:7, ESV). Just as this world was redeemed by the blood of Christ, so too Narnia was saved by the blood of Aslan, the Narnian Christ.

In the second epistle of Peter (3:3), he writes: "Knowing this first, that there shall come in the last days scoffers, walking after their own lusts." At the last days of Narnia, too, there are scoffers: the Dwarfs. In chapter seven, we see the true colors of this small band. They tell the group of Narnians: "We've no more use for stories about Aslan" (page 90). Later they say: "We're on our own now. The Dwarfs are for the Dwarfs" (page 91). As in our world, Narnia has its scoffers of the truth. The Dwarfs follow after their desires, and thus miss the truth, just as Peter referred to in the above verse.

After this comes a very distinct reference to Scripture. Again we meet the skeptical Dwarfs, who insist that Shift show them what is really in the stable. "Come on, Monkey, show us what's in the stable, see is believing." This points back quite clearly to John 20:25, when the disciples tell Thomas they have seen Jesus risen from the dead. Thomas does not believe, but says: "Except I shall see in his hands the print of the nails, and put my finger into the print of the nails...I will not believe." In both cases of doubt, the result was the same. Thomas met Jesus face to face; the Dwarfs were thrown into the stable and meet the real Aslan. But the response is very different: Thomas is willing to repent of his doubt, becoming a true disciple again. The Dwarfs, though given the chance, stay blind to the truth because they can't let go of their pride.

In the same chapter we find a beautiful picture of how God cares for His children. When the Narnians are facing a very deadly and Evil force, Tirian encourages the small group with these words: "But courage, child: we are all between the paws of the true Aslan" (page 134). The Bible gives a similar mental image of God's protection of us in Deuteronomy 33:27: "The eternal God is your dwelling place, and underneath are the everlasting arms."

When the Ape is recognized for what he is, the stable he had been using for the false god Tash (and filling his pockets because of it) becomes Shift's destruction. When Tirian throws him into it, the Ape finds that Tash really does exist, and is destroyed by the corruption he had brought to Narnia. This is an obvious example of how using evil to further your purposes can turn on you, something the Bible makes very clear. It is likely that Lewis had 2 Peter 2:12 in mind when he created this part of the story: "But these, as natural brute beasts, made to be taken and destroyed, speak evil of the things that they understand not; and shall utterly perish in their own corruption." This is certainly what happened to

Shift.

Notice also that the Narnians pass into the New Narnia by way of a door (similar in numerous respects to the ways they came into Narnia from our world in the books LWW and SC). This is quite like one of the sayings of Jesus: "I am the door: by me if any man enter in, he shall be saved, and shall go in and out, and find pasture" (John 10:9).

When the children go through the stable door, they find the Dwarfs who had refused to side with them. But instead of realizing they are in the New Narnia, the Dwarfs believe they are locked in the stable. If they would but put their prejudices aside and believe Aslan, they could be welcomed into the New Narnia. Instead, they continue to think they are stuck in a simple stable, with no hope. Aslan tries to make them see, but they refuse. Aslan says of them: "They will not let us help them. They have chosen cunning instead of belief. Their prison is only in their own minds, yet they are in that prison, and so afraid of being taken in that they cannot be taken out" (page 186). In one of His teachings, Jesus described some people who are just like those Dwarfs: "...seeing they do not see, and hearing they do not hear, nor do they understand....For this people's heart has grown dull, and with their ears they can barely hear, and their eyes they have closed, lest they should see with their eyes and hear with their ears and understand with their heart and turn, and I would heal them" (Matthew 13:13, 15 ESV).

Numerous skeptics of Lewis' theology have claimed that he did not believe in a literal Hell, basing their claim on an obscure passage from his short novel *The Great Divorce*. As this discussion is limited to the Narniad, we will not get into the details. Let it suffice to say that Scripture makes it quite clear that there is a literal

Hell, a place just as real as Heaven. Lewis firmly believed in Hell, dedicating an entire chapter in his book, *The Problem of Pain*, to the subject.

The reason I mention this is that in LB we see a realistic portrayal of both Heaven and Hell. In chapter 12 of LB, we get our second look at the god Tash, which is the Narnian form of Satan (as is the White Witch). At this last battle, Tirian throws himself and Rishda into the stable. It is clear that the stable is a form of death, like passing through death's door. What is on the other side is fascinating. Tirian finds himself in a beautiful paradise; the Calormen general, on the other hand, finds himself face to face with the demon Tash. Lewis describes the scene on page 166:

> With a sudden jerk…Tash pounced on the miserable Rishda and tucked him under the upper of his two arms. Then Tash turned his head sidewise to fix Tirian with one of his terrible eyes…
>
> But immediately, from behind Tash, strong and calm as the summer sea, a voice said:
>
> 'Begone, Monster, and take your lawful prey to your own place: in the name of Aslan and Aslan's great Father the Emperor-over-the-sea.'

This part of the story makes it clear that evil in Narnia has its "own place", just as in this world. Note the fact that Lewis uses the term "lawful prey". According to the laws of Aslan, Rishda was Tash's to take. This parallels closely with the Biblical teachings of justice: in our world, there is a place of judgment after death, a place called Hell; all evil will one day be punished. It appears, from the above quote, that Narnia has the same sense of justice. Rishda gave himself over to idol worship and received what he wanted. It is also of importance to note that this same punishment of evil is touched on in LWW. The White Witch correctly states that all traitors are hers by right. It is only through Aslan's death that this law can be satisfied. At the final end of Narnia, there is a last judgment by Aslan of all creatures of that world. Each come through the doorway and look straight into the face of Aslan:

> I don't think they had a choice about that. And when some looked, the expression of their faces changed terribly—it was fear and hatred: except for that, on the faces of the Talking Beasts, the fear and hatred lasted only for a fraction of a second. You could see that they suddenly ceased to be *Talking* Beasts. They were just ordinary animals. And all the creatures who looked at Aslan in that way swerved to their right, his left, and disappeared into his huge black shadow which...streamed away to the left of the doorway. The children never saw them again. But the other looked into the face of Aslan and loved him, though some of them were very frightened at the same time. And all these came in at the Door, in on Aslan's right (page 193).

Marvin Hinten makes an interesting point on this part of the story: "The evil creatures depart to Aslan's left; the good creatures to his right. This accords with the biblical parting of the "sheep and the goats" (good and evil) of Matthew 25:33 'And he shall set the sheep on his right hand, but the goats on the left.'"[81]

The end of the Narnian world has numerous direct

parallels to those prophesied for our planet. After the judgment discussed above, Narnia goes through its last stages of demise. As we read this component of the story, it becomes clear to anyone with a knowledge of end times that Lewis leaned heavily on the Bible for inspiration. After Tirian passes through the stable door, he finds himself in Aslan's country; and instead of the old, war-tattered clothes he was wearing he finds that: "He was fresh and cool and clean, and dressed in such clothes as he would have worn for a great feast" (page 167). This is a reflection of the biblical teaching Paul discussed in one of his letters: "Behold! I tell you a mystery. We shall not all sleep, but we shall all be changed" (1 Corinthians 15:51). After death there will be significant changes for all mankind; as we can see, Narnia is no different.

On the other side of the Door is perhaps the most obvious reference to the Bible. Shortly after Tirian goes through the Door Lucy is explaining how the inside of the Stable is bigger than the outside. She then says: "In our world too, a stable once had something inside it that was bigger than our whole world" (page 177). This could point only back to the birth of Christ in a stable; as God Himself, he was bigger than our entire universe, yet still fit in the stable walls.

When Tirian meets Aslan for the first time, in the New Narnia, the great Lion says these familiar words: "Well done, last of the Kings of Narnia who stood firm at the darkest hour" (LB, page 183). The above is exactly like the blessing God gives all His faithful servants on the other side of death: "His lord [referring to God] said unto him, 'Well done, thou good and faithful servant: thou hast been faithful over a few things, I will make thee ruler over many things: enter thou into the joy of thy lord'" (Matthew

25:21).

In chapter fourteen the actual end of the Old Narnia begins. Almost right away we notice something we've seen before: "Immediately the sky became full of shooting stars. Even one shooting star is a fine thing to see; but these were dozens, and then scores… till it was like a silver rain: and it went on and on…. All the stars were falling: Aslan was calling them home" (page 189). This is exactly what the Bible describes as what will happen at the end of our world: "But in those days, after that tribulation… the stars of heaven shall fall, and the powers that are in heaven shall be shaken" (Mark 13:25).

Besides this, there are other signs in the heavens that are associated with the end of Narnia as well as our world. One example is the following: "Then the Moon came up, quite in her wrong position, very close to the sun, and she also looked red" (page 196). The prophet Joel talked about an event just like this: "The sun shall be turned to darkness, and the moon to blood, before the great and awesome day of the LORD comes" (Joel 2:31 ESV; the New Testament mentions the same thing in Revelation 6:12).

Perhaps one of the most central things Lewis brought out in his writing discussing Heaven was not only that it was a very real place, but in fact was even more real than this world we now live in. He considered earth to be but a shadow in comparison to the New Heavens and New Earth.[82] The New Narnia is no different; it is very much like the old, yet somehow more real: "The new one was a deeper country: every rock and flower and blade of grass looked as if it meant more" (page 213). Just as in Narnia, we are looking forward to a New Heavens and New Earth. And we can be sure it will truly make this world look like a shadow, just as the New Narnia made the old one look. One verse that talks of this is 2 Peter 3:13: "But according to his promise we are waiting for new heavens and a new earth in which righteousness dwells."

As the Narnians discovered, and we long for, Aslan's country is the true country; all others are just copies or shadows of it. And this sums the whole of what Heaven is to be like.[83]

Conclusion

Many doubt that the Bible had much of an effect on the creation of this series; however, the evidence covered in this chapter should be sufficient to lay such claims to rest. The reader must also bear in mind that this chapter was in no way exhaustive; because of space limits much has been left out. Not even addressed are the presence of Biblical values through the books that, though do not refer back to one specific verse in the Bible, have their roots in it. Among these virtues are such things as courage, honor, mercy, love, compassion, fairness, nobility, and many others. In fact, these characteristics appear so often that we could easily fill a book with them.

The general conclusion of the matter is thus: though the Bible played a large role in the formation of the series, this was not Lewis' purpose. Rather, Biblical truths are woven within the storyline in a subtle fashion, without preaching to his reader. In fact, as discussed in chapter one, Lewis first formed the story and as he wrote it, the theological elements worked their way into it on their own accord.

Many people make the mistake of reading the Narniad and searching for a Bible verse behind every line. This is unfortunate in two ways: for one, most of the time they aren't there; and for another, it tends to cause the reader to add things to the story, coming to a completely different view than what the Chronicles were intended to be for. When a person tries to make a parable out of a story, they lose the story itself in the process.

In summary, there is much Biblical truth to be gleaned from the Chronicles. However, we must recognize them first and foremost as quality stories, not Christian allegories. Too often we try to allegorize everything and along the way miss the story for what it is.

Chapter Four

Random Objections and "Problems" in the
Chronicles of Narnia

In this chapter, we will look at a collection of 'problems' in the Narniad. Basically, this chapter will cover those that did not get answered in the previous chapters. As we have seen, and will continue to see, most of the problems skeptics raise against the Chronicles are untrue, misinterpreted, or out of context.

Racism in Narnia

In discussing the objections to the Narniad, one of my cousins said: "The Calormenes wore turbans, lived in the desert, worshipped the devil, and were dark skinned." His argument was that Lewis was implying racism. It can't be denied that the Narnian 'good guys' are white-skinned people from England. The Calormenes were obviously dark-skinned and hateful enemies of

Aslan and Narnia (HHB, p. 3).

It also is apparent that the nation of Calormen was intended to be Eastern in its culture, location, etc. Although this is possibly the case, there are some false theories and untruths in this argument, and as we will see, this is not racism as we think of it.

First, the Calormenes do not live in the Great Desert that separates the Calormen from Archenland and Narnia. Although it was most likely more warm there then in Narnia (considering its southern location), Calormen is basically the same geographically, though with a flatter landscape.

Unfortunately, the Calormenes do seem to be modeled after the Muslims. However, before we say this that means Lewis was a racist, please understand the context of the story and the time Lewis was alive. Paul Ford explains it well:

> C. S. Lewis was a man of his time and socioeconomic class. Like many Englishman of his era, Lewis was unconsciously but regrettably unsympathetic to the things and people Middle Eastern. Thus he sometimes engages in exaggerated stereotyping in contrasting things Narnian and Calormene. He intends this in a broadly comic way, almost vaudevillian. But in our post-September 11, 2001, world, he would, I am sure, want to reconsider this insensitivity.[84]

Although what Ford said is the case, Lewis never said that the people of Calormen were lower in value then the Narnians. Rather, it seems more that he was saying they were need of being freed from the false god Tash, just like the Muslims of today need to be freed by Jesus Christ.

Also of important note, in the quote above about this being just part of the culture of the day, is that something very much like racism appears in the beloved classic, *Pilgrim's Progress*. In that volume, Bunyan goes out of his way to say that one of the evil characters is black. The black man leads Christian and Hopeful into a trap, and it turns out he works against all Christians.[85] However, this was just the culture of the day, when Christians often called Africa tribes brutes, savages, and pagans. Thankfully, this has changed over the last century.

And of course, it is logical that such two different people groups would be enemies. Indeed, Lewis wrote in his 'Narnian Timeline' that the Calormenes were the ancestors of outcasts from Archenland, which proves beyond doubt that they and Narnians are of the same race (that is, Adam's) and are equals.

In fact, there is nothing in the Chronicles that suggest that Calormenes are not equal to Narnians. The fact they have dark skin is logical since they live south of Narnia in a warmer climate, just as Arabs are south of England (where Lewis lived).

Salvation is offered and available to Calormenes, such as in the case of Rabadash and Emeth. Rabadash refused the mercy Aslan offered him and paid the consequences (HHB, page 233-236). Emeth, however, is saved and goes to the Narnian Heaven (LB, page 201-206).

The most obvious example of the fact that the Calormenes are equals with the Narnians, however, would be the one of Aravis, which is one of the major themes of HBB. Aravis is treated as equal to Narnians and is even asked to come live in the castle of Anvard with the rest of the Archenland royalty. She later marries Prince, and later King, Cor, the son of King Lune. She gave birth to Ram the Great, which later became the greatest of Archenland's kings.

Lewis expressed in his own writing that he was not racist:

> In any mind which has a pennyworth of imagination it produces a good attitude towards foreigners. How can I love my home without coming to realize that other men, no less rightly, love theirs? Once you have realized that the Frenchmen like café complet just as we like bacon and eggs—why, good luck to them and let them have it. [The] last thing we want is to make everywhere else just like our own home.[86]

There is nothing in the Chronicles that suggests racism. The relationship between Narnia and Calormen can be compared to the children of Israel and the surrounding countries. The Israelite's enemies could be saved, though few turned from their sins. This isn't racism. In the same way, Aslan wasn't favoring certain people groups. Salvation was open to the Calormenes. Some chose it (Aravis), others did not (Rabadash).

Why was C. S. Lewis 'Ashamed' of His Beliefs?

It has been said (even mentioned when I was discussing this with a friend) that if Lewis wanted to write a Christian story, why didn't he just come out and say it instead of hiding the Christian symbolism?

First of all, Lewis was not 'ashamed' to say his beliefs. A quick reading of his *Mere Christianity* or *The Problem of Pain* rapidly shows this idea to be false. But why would Lewis hid the Christian symbols so well in the Chronicles of Narnia?

There is a good reason for doing so. Firstly, remember he was simply trying to write a wholesome children's story, not an allegory (see chapter one). This is one reason why it is so subtle.

Secondly, it is important to note that if he would have made the Narnia tales outright allegories (not simply analogies), the volume of readers of the Chronicles would have been significantly lower (over 100 million copies of the Narnia books have been sold in 47 languages).[87]

It is important to note the difference between allegory and analogy.[88] An allegory is an intentional retelling of something, as in the case of *Pilgrim's Progress*, which is an allegory of the walk of every Christian. An analogy is more hidden in its symbolism. Although it is still there, they are usually not the main focus of the story. This is what Lewis is doing in the Narniad.

Also note that the Christian symbols in these books are not really that hidden. If you keep a sharp eye out for them, they start popping up all throughout the series. This has already been discussed in chapter three.

Doesn't the Narniad Teach Astrology?

Another thing skeptics often mention is what looks like something similar to astrology in the Narnia tales. It is quite obvious from a quick reading of the series that the stars were used to tell 'the signs of the times'. Indeed, the centaurs are known for their watching of the heavens (PC, page 82; LB, pages 18-19).

But before we go into what the Narnia stories say about this and if this is a reasonable objection, we will first take a brief look at what astrology is and teaches.

According to Webster's dictionary, the word *astrology* means "a method or theory based on the assumption that the positions of the moon, sun, and stars affect human affairs and can foretell the future." In other words, the positions of the stars can be used as fortune tellers (this is the most common form of this theory; others may include the sun and moon, but this is not what is talked about in the Narniad, and is therefore irrelevant).

According to World Book Encyclopedia, astrology was first developed in Babylon around 2000 B.C., which would have been shortly after the Genesis Flood in the days of Noah. Later, about 1000 B.C., they adopted the Zodiac, which are the twelve signs/constellations that are used to predict future events and are used to decide various things about a person's character and personality. For example, if you are born between June 21 and July 22, you have the constellation Cancer as your Zodiac 'sign' and your personality will be emotional, patriotic and home loving. At least, according to the astrologers. This is how this practice works. Although the whole system probably started as a simple superstition, it has now become wrapped up in Satanic and occult practices.[89] As Christians we know from the start that the Bible condemns practicing astrology (Isaiah 47:13-15; Deuteronomy 4:19). So now the question arises, doesn't the Chronicles of Narnia talk about this superstition, and if so, is this not enough to prove they are not Christian and are in fact dangerous?

There are basically two references to things similar to astrology is the series. The first is in PC, page 82: "'The time is ripe,' said Glenstorm [a centaur]. 'I watch the skies, Badger, for it is my to watch, as it is your to remember. Tarva and Alambil have met in the halls of high heaven, and on earth a son of Adam has once more arisen to rule and name the creatures. The hour has struck.'"

The second reference is in LB, pages 18-19: "'Sire,' he [Roonwit, a centaur] said. 'You know how long I have lived and studied the stars... Never in all my days have I seen such terrible things written in the skies as there have been nightly since this year began. The stars say nothing of Aslan, nor of peace, nor of joy. I know by my art that there has never been such a disastrous conjunctions of the planets for five hundred years. ...The stars never lie...'"

In the land of Narnia, centaurs are known for star watching and their ability to prophecy certain events. For example, in HB (pages 220-221) Shasta is taken to an old, wise centaur shortly after he is born. The centaur then foretells that he would later save Narnia and Archenland from a great danger (which he does by warning both countries of an attack by Prince Rabadash of Calormen).

From the examples given above, it seems quite clear the Narniad teaches astrology as something the 'good guys' do. At least, that's what it seems to be, but let's look at this in more detail.

First of all, it is important to know what astrology means now and what it meant to Lewis sixty years ago. Astrology is occultic and has many recognized problems scientifically. No doubt Lewis himself also held this view. However, as stated earlier, what is true in our world may not be the case in another world. For example, the Narnian world is flat instead of a sphere like ours.

It is also of great importance to note that the Narnia series is in a medieval-type setting. Remember that in the Middle Ages, astrology was considered a science, just like astronomy today. They also believed the world was flat and that all the planets went around the sun. What Lewis does is take those ideas once thought to be scientific and makes them a reality in a different world. So in Narnia, one finds things that are proven myths in this world to be real things in that world. These include the flat earth, mythological creatures, and astrology. This is one reason this objection is not valid.

Another important thing to remember is that signs in the heavens are really a biblical concept. Examples of God using astronomical bodies to signal certain events are found in both the Old and New Testaments. These would include the rainbow after Noah's Flood (Genesis 9:12-16), and the wise men following the star, which was the sign of Jesus' birth (Matthew 2:2, 9-11). Also, the end of this world will be accompanied by certain heavenly signs (Joel 2:10, 30; 3:15). So when Lewis uses the stars to tell about events going on in Narnia, it seems likely that he is just following the examples given in Scripture. This is clear in the case in LB where catastrophic signs in the heavens signal the end of the world. We know from the book of Joel that this will be the case in our world. Lewis was probably simply copying these passages. It seems plausible that the centaurs and their star gazing is a spinoff of the wise men in Matthew 2.

There is one last thing to note before we leave this topic. Never once in the Chronicles are stars used to actually tell of future events. They only accompany them. This is very important to remember because, by definition, astrology is using astronomical object to tell the future. This is not what happens in Narnia.

The Stone Table and Occult Sacrifices

One thing skeptics sometimes bring up is that the sacrifice of Aslan on the Stone Table is connected with pagan rituals and has its origins in occult practices. In reality, this idea doesn't hold water.

In the Narnian symbolism, Aslan is crafted after Christ. Aslan willingly gives his life in Edmund's place to satisfy the ancient laws that rule that world. The parallels with the Gospel story are obvious.

Skeptics say that this part of the story is modeled more after pagan rituals than after the crucifixion of Jesus. Although it does borrow from some ancient myths, it is still centered on the Scriptures. Many things about this are simply too close to the Bible's account to be a coincidence (the previous chapter covers the exact spiritual significance of this part of the Narniad). When carefully considered, Aslan dying on the Stone Table is really no more pagan and 'unchristian' than the Crucifixion. Jesus died on a pagan, Roman cross at the hands of cruel and ungodly soldiers. The crucifixion was completely different from the sacrifices that the children of Israel did to cover their sins. The average person watching Jesus die on the Cross would have said it had more in common with pagan executions than with blood shed to wash away sins. The point of all this is to show that Jesus' death was very much pagan in many ways, so why should we get so upset at the Narnian 'style' of Jesus' sacrifice because it is partly based in the realm of mythological?

One thing to also notice is that the skeptics never give a detailed description of why it is similar to ungodly practices. Remember too that C. S. Lewis was not trying to write an allegory, only a good children's story with some Christian symbolism mixed in. One would not expect the death of Aslan to be modeled entirely from Scripture. When we realize this, it is not hard to see why Lewis borrowed some pagan tradition and myths for the Stone Table sacrifice.

What about Adam's Race Healing Narnia?

One thing critics often bring up is a statement Aslan makes in MN: "And as Adam's race has done the harm, Adam's race shall it help heal it" (page 162).

But is that theologically sound? After all, it is Jesus who has healed this world of evil, not the humans.

It is important to note that Lewis has Aslan say Adam's race shall *help* heal Narnia. It is Aslan who really saves Narnia in the end; humans were simply one of the tools he used. This is quite clear in LWW. It is Aslan who breaks the spell of winter and kills the White Witch. The four children only help in this process. This principle is also true in our lives, and I wonder if Lewis was intentionally teaching this. We are humble tools in God's hands. Often he uses us to reach out to the lost souls of this world, but it he who really saves them. We just point them in the right direction. In a way, we are helping to undo the evil that the first man, Adam, brought into the world. When viewed from this angle, there is nothing wrong with this quote from MN.

On the References to Wine and Beer in the Chronicles

Even to the most casual reader of the Narniad, the mentions of wine and beer can't be missed. There are frequent references to such strong drinks in many places throughout the series. Scripture has much to say against over consumption of alcoholic beverages, so how can reconcile the Bible with this part of Narnia?

First, remember the culture and time setting when Lewis wrote the Chronicles. In England sixty years ago, it was the accepted thing to go have a pint of ale with your friends at the local pub. For Lewis, this meant that hanging out at a pub for a few drinks was fine. Though at first glance this seems very un-Christian, note that in this case, drinking a pint of beer was not for the purpose of getting drunk. Rather, it would be just like going to a coffee shop, which is becoming a hangout place just like the pubs of Lewis' day.[90]

Secondly, never once in the Narnia series does the use of wine or beer ever reach the point of excess and drunkenness, except in the case of Puddleglum, who drinks a giant's form of beer, which is much stronger than he anticipated. In fact, the Narnia tales paint a dark picture for those who cannot control their use of wine. Uncle Andrew, a decidedly anti-Narnian character, has a strong weakness for brandy (MN, page 88).

Third, this objection does not stand because of the fact

that the use of wine is also in the Bible. The most obvious example would be the first recorded miracle of Jesus, where He turned water into wine. It was such good wine that the person in charge wondered why the best was given at the end of the wedding.

And lastly, we must consider what Lewis wrote on this topic, and how the way we view wine has changed. Lewis wrote the following in his book *Mere Christianity*, when discussing the subject of temperance:

> Temperance is, unfortunately, one of those words that has changed its meaning…. Temperance referred not specially to drink, but to all pleasures; and it meant not abstaining, but going the right length and no further…. An individual Christian may see fit to give up all sorts of things for special reasons—marriage, or meat, or beer, or the cinema; but the moment he starts saying the things are bad in themselves, or looking down his nose at other people who do use them, he has taken the wrong turning.[91]

Lewis was well aware that legitimate pleasures God had given us could be abused. He watched his brother, Warren, struggle for many years with alcoholism, which could explain why he shows the dangers of drunkenness in various plotlines of the Narniad.

We must take into account the time setting of the Chronicles. Consider the following:

> …his stories reflect the times in which they are set— approximately the Middle Ages. As a specialist in medieval

literature, Lewis was familiar with the prevalence of and attitudes toward wine and beer consumption in that era. Back then, wine was considered a food staple, and safer to drink than the often bacteria-laden water. Beverages brewed from grains were thick and relatively nutritious, and their alcohol content tended to be lower. Mead, a mildly alcoholic brew made from honey, was distributed liberally to all ages. (Distilled alcohol came along hundreds of years later.)

As in many times and cultures, including our own, alcohol then was supposed to have medicinal qualities. On board the Dawn Treader, Prince Caspian pulls the children from cold seas, then offers them hot spiced wine as a warmer (Eustace grumbles that he'd rather have a vitamin preparation). Think of this kind of imbibing as the cough syrup...of the day.[92]

If we look carefully at what the Bible says, it becomes clear that wine and other similar drinks are not condemned. Rather, it is drunkenness that is the sin. A quick reading of Proverbs makes it very plain. Though Lewis did drink beer, never is he known to have gotten drunk. He knew his limits and realized it was a sin. As far as we can see, the Narniad does not contradict the Bible in this area.

Who is Lilith and what is Her Significance?

A very interesting part of the LWW is the discussion of the four Pevensies and the Beavers. In this, the children are introduced to their first look at what Narnia really is: an enslaved country. In this conversation the question comes up as to who the White

Witch is and if she is human. Mr. Beaver provides them with this answer:

'She'd like us to believe it [that she is human],' said Mr. Beaver, 'and it's on that that she bases her claim to be Queen.

'But she's no Daughter of Eve. She comes from your father Adam's...first wife, they called her Lilith. And she was one of the Jinn. That's what she comes from on one side. And on the other she comes of the giants. No, no, there isn't a drop of real human blood in the Witch' (LWW, page 87-88).

Who is this Lilith that Lewis is talking about?

Lilith was a mythological figure in Babylonian and Hebrew traditions. She was considered to be a female demon that killed newborn babies and haunted the forest searching for children (not exactly a pleasant character). In the LWW, she is one of the Jinn, who were spirits that could take on various forms appearances.[93] Lilith is said to be the mother of the White Witch, which explains why the Witch spends most of the book trying to capture the Pevensie children.[94]

Why did Lewis include this in the story? Doesn't this teach bad theology? In a word, no. Lilith was included in the book for exactly the same reason that there are fauns, centaurs, and dwarves. He never intended for these mythological elements of the story to be taken seriously. On the contrary, his goal was to weave a good children's book that included things that are myths. Skeptics who say that this shows Lewis had weird theology should take the time to realize that many things in the Narnia series do not reflect things he thought were reality. This part of the story is to be taken no more as fact then the talking animals. Lilith is added simply to put an interesting flavor and fairy tale aspect to this book.

What about Emeth in the Last Battle?

Admittedly, this is one of the most difficult and serious objection put forward. Honestly, I don't believe we will know the full answer to this complex subject.

This part of the story is just after the end of Narnia when the main characters are exploring the new Narnia, which is a form of Heaven. Shortly they meet Emeth, who is (was) a Calormene and had served Tash. He enter the sable door because of his interest in meeting "Tashlan," a strange mixture of Tash and Aslan that the Calormenes used to deceive the Narnians. Here Emeth recounts his story of seeing Aslan for the first time in the new Narnia.

> [When I saw him]…I fell at his feet and thought, Surely this is the hour of death, for the Lion (who is worthy of all honor) will know that I have served Tash all my days and not him. Nevertheless, it is better to see the Lion and die than to be Tisroc [a Calormen king] if the world and live and not to have seen him. But the Glorious One bent down his golden head and touched my forehead with his tongue and said, Son, thou art welcome. But I said, Alas, Lord, I am no son of thine but the servant of Tash. He answered, Child, all the service thou hast done to Tash, I account as service done to me. … [I] said, Lord, is it then true…that thou and Tash are one? The Lion growled

so that the earth shook (but his wrath was not against me) and said, It is false. Not because he and I are one, but because we are opposites, I take to me the services which thou hast done to him. For I and he are of such different kinds that no service which is vile can be done to me, and none which is not vile can be done to him. Therefore, if any man swear by Tash and keep his oath for the oath's sake, it is by me that he has truly sworn, though he know it not, and it is I who reward him. And if any man do a cruelty in my name, then, though he says the name Aslan, it is Tash whom he serves and by Tash his deed is accepted.... But I said…, Yet I have been seeking Tash all my days. Beloved, said the Glorious One, unless thy desire had been for me thou wouldst not have sought so long and so truly. For all find what they truly seek (LB, pages 204-206).

How can a man who has served Tash (the Satan figure in Narnia) all his life be accepted by Aslan (the Christ figure) as if his deeds had been for him?

A quick and almost too easy answer is one already mentioned: that of the fact that Lewis was simply writing a good book for children and not an allegory. Therefore, many of the things in this series are not to be taken literally, or as a reflection of his personal beliefs. It could be argued that Lewis put this part in the story just to give the book a happy ending all around, since Emeth was a very noble person who wanted to really know the truth. Interestingly, the name Emeth is the Hebrew word for "faithful, true." We know that Lewis was aware of this and intentionally used this name to match the character; in his book *The Abolition of Man* he discusses the meaning of this name.[95]

Though that is a simply solution to the problem, I believe it runs much deeper than that. Lewis spends an entire chapter on this in the book, and since an author's beliefs often are reflected in their novels, there must be more to this than just a simply story.

It is interesting to note that skeptics are quick to point out all the different theological errors in the above section, yet seem to miss the truth also contained in it. As I studied this more in depth, I found that if we take a look at the part of this that is Biblically correct, we find the problem is more easily explained.

The last two sentences in the above section are critical: "… unless thy desire had been for me thou wouldst not have sought so long and so truly. For all find what they truly seek."

Every sane human being is looking for something, which is why there are so many religions in the world today. People want to be filled with something that really satisfies. What most do not know is that what they are looking for is really God Himself, who is the only answer to man's greatest problem. Here Lewis brilliantly brings this to life with the Calormene religion. They were searching for something, but turned to the wrong person. The answer was Aslan. What Lewis is saying is that this is the driving force behind all religions: a search for God but coming to the wrong answer. This was Emeth's problem. He then started to believe that maybe Tash and Aslan were one. With the motive of finding the truth, he entered the sable door in search of the One True God. Instead of finding Tash, Emeth met Aslan, who welcomed him as his own.

Lewis is here painting a picture of someone held captive by religion, which is sincerely looking for the truth, but ended up with The Truth finding them. An example could be a Muslim who believes he is following God while worshipping Allah. In his search for meaning and truth, he comes to believe that Allah and the Christian God are one. Though this is not entirely correct, he is coming closer to the Ultimate Truth: God himself. This Muslim may hold this belief for some time, until he comes face-to-face with God, as Emeth came face-to-face with Aslan. Then he realizes that his service to Allah was false, and in reality was just searching for God his whole life, perhaps without even knowing it. This is what Lewis seems to be getting at, though some of the parts in this story are still unclear. (For example, service done to Tash is counted as service done to Aslan.) These are confusing, yes, but the general argument that Aslan was letting an idol-worshipper into Heaven is false.

This appears to not be a serious problem that means the series is hopelessly wandered from the Bible. In fact, one person I talked with concerning this believed the Chronicles to be unholy reading because of this very thing. He then went on to reject all of Lewis' writing out of hand.

Conclusion

When examined closely, these issues can easily be explained. Even the ones where the answer is not entirely satisfactory, the objection is not a big enough problem to really make an issue out of it.

There are no simple answers to the complex issues raised by the fictional works of C. S. Lewis. This does not mean, however, that the meaning cannot be determined. Rather, Lewis has left many clues for us to follow. Those who accuse the Chronicles of Narnia of being unchristian, teaching poor theology, or even of teaching witchcraft are misinformed and have not taken the time to study out their true meaning, nor put forth the effort to understand the complex backdrop of their origins. Those who give quick, cookie-cutter answers condemning Narnia have not taken the time to fully grasp the setting in which they were created. This should serve as a lesson in being cautious when casting judging; these issues are rarely as simple and straightforward as some make them appear.

Works Cited

(Endnotes)

1. Devin Brown, *Exploring Narnia* (Grand Rapids, MI: BakerBooks, 2005), page 14.
2. Mary van Nattan. Retrieved from http://www.jesus-is-savior.com/Wolves/cs_lewis-fool.htm.
3. In this book we will always use the order that the books were published, not the order they are now sold in (which is MN, LWW, HHB, PC, VDT, SC, LB). Though this is not necessarily the exact order they were written in, the original order of publication better shows the progression of themes, characters, and, most importantly, the growth of Lewis as a children's writer and master of literature.
4. Lewis, *An Experiment in Criticism* (Cambridge, UK: Cambridge University Press, 1961), page 121.
5. Lewis, *A Preface to Paradise Lost* (New York, NY: Oxford University Press, 1942), page 1.
6. Paul Ford, *in* Schultz and West, *The C. S. Lewis Readers Encyclopedia* (Grand Rapids, MI: ZondervanPublishingHouse, 1998), page 121.
7. Colin Duriez, *The C. S. Lewis Encyclopedia* (Wheaton, IL: Crossway Books, 2000), page 67.
8. Lewis, *Of Other Worlds* (New York, NY: Harcourt, Brace & World, Inc., 1966), page 42.
9. Lewis, *The Letters of C. S. Lewis: Revised and Enlarged Edition* (New York, NY: Harvest Books, 1988), page 486.
10. Lewis, *Of Other Worlds*, page 36.
11. George Sayer. *Jack: A Life of C. S. Lewis* (Wheaton, IL: Crossway Books, 1994 [second edition]), page 318.
12. *Of Other Worlds*, page 88.
13. Charles Brady, review of the *Last Battle* in *America* (October 27, 1956).
14. Lewis, quoted in Walter Hooper, *C. S. Lewis: Companion and Guide* (New

York, NY: HarperSanFrancisco, 1996), page 209.

15. Ibid, page 424.

16. Ibid, page 425.

17. Lewis, *The Letters of C. S. Lewis: Revised and Enlarged Edition*, page 475-6.

18. Ibid, page 486. Letter dated December 24, 1959, to Sophia Storr.

19. Lewis, *Reflections on the Psalms* (New York, NY: Harvest Book/Harcourt, Inc., 1958), pages 99-100.

20. *Of Other Worlds*, pages 57-58

21. Lewis, quoted in Schultz and West, *The C. S. Lewis Readers Encyclopedia* (Grand Rapids, MI: ZondervanPublishingHouse, 1998), page 109.

22. Lee Stobel and Garry Poole, *Exploring the Da Vinci Code* (Grand Rapids, MI: Zondervan, 2006), page 8.

23. Pullman, quoted in Richard Abanes, *Harry Potter, Narnia, and the Lord of the Rings* (Eugene, OR: Harvest House Publishers, 2005), page 37.

24. Ted Dekker, *The Slumber of Christianity* (Nashville, TN: Thomas Nelson Publishers, 2004), page 141-142.

25. Ray Vander Laan lecture, Feb. 10, 2012, Maryville TN.

26. N. T. Wright, *The New Testament and the People of God* (Minneapolis, MN: Fortress Press, 1992), page 372.

27. Terry Glaspey, *The Spiritual Legacy of C. S. Lewis* (Nashville, TN: Cumberland House, 1996), pages 47-48.

28. Lewis, *Out of the Silent Planet* (New York, NY: The Macmillan Company, 1967) page 167.

29. Kathryn Lindskoog, *Surprised by C. S. Lewis, George MacDonald, and Dante: An Array of Original Discoveries* (Macon, GA: Mercer University Press, 2001), page 173.

30. Lewis, *George MacDonald: An Anthology 365 Readings* (New York, NY: Harper Collins Publishers, Inc., 2001), page xxxviii.

31. Alister McGrath, *C. S. Lewis: A Life* (Carol Stream, IL: Tyndale House Publishers, 2013), page 260.

32. Lewis, *The Letters of C. S. Lewis: Revised and Enlarged Edition*, pages 445-6. Letter to Mrs. Ashton, February 2, 1955.

33. C. N. Manlove, quoted in Abanes, *Harry Potter, Narnia, and the Lord of the Rings*, page 19.

34. Lewis, *Surprised by Joy* (New York, NY: Harcourt, Inc, 1955), page 59-60.

35. Ibid, page 82.

36. *Of Other Worlds*, page 28-30.

37. Abanes, page 144.

38. Sarah Arthur, *Walking through the Wardrobe* (Wheaton, IL: Tyndale House Publishers, 2005), pages xvii-xviii.

39. Madeleine L'Engle, *Bright Evening Star* (Wheaton, IL: Harold Shaw Publishers, 1997), pages 55-56.

40. *C. S. Lewis: A Life*, pages 263-264.

41. Lewis, *George MacDonald: An Anthology* (New York, NY: HarperOne Publishers, 2001 [originally published 1946]), page xxxviii.

42. Oswald Chambers, edited by James Riemann, *My Utmost for His Highest*, (Grand Rapids, MI: Discovery House Publishers, 1992 updated edition). February 10th entry.

43. Sayers, *Letters to a Diminished Church* (Nashville, TN: Thomas Nelson Publishers, 2004), page 1.

44. Ibid, page 48.

45. *Of Other Worlds*, page 37.

46. *The Abolition of Man* in *The Complete C. S. Lewis Signature Classics* (New York, NY: HarperOne Publishers, 2002), page 728.

47. *The Collected Letters of C. S. Lewis: Books, Broadcasts, and the War* (New York, NY: HarperSanFrancisco, 2004), pages 841-842.

48. *The Abolition of Man*, page 726.

49. *The Screwtape Letters* in *Ibid*, page 183.

50. Lewis, *Surprised by Joy* (Orlando, FL: Harcourt Books, 1955), page 60.

51. *The Weight of Glory and Other Addresses* (New York, NY: HarperOne Publishers, 1980), page 111.

52. Richard Abanes, *Harry Potter, Narnia, and Lord of the Rings* (Eugene, OR: Harvest House Publishers, 2005), page 99.

53. Marcus Brotherton, "The Meaning of Magic in Narnia" *in* Heather and David Kopp, *Roar: A Christian Family Guide to the Chronicles of Narnia* (Sisters, OR: Multnamah Publishers, 2005), page 338.

54. *Letters to Malcolm: Chiefly on Prayer* (New York, NY: Mariner Books, 2012 [originally published 1964]), pages 102-104.

55. Some have question this interpretation of Aslan's identity. However, it is abundantly clear from Lewis's own writings that this is what he indented with the character of Aslan. See for example his *Letters to Children* (London: Collins/Fount Paperbacks, 1985), pages 32, 52-53, etc.

56. One could possibly argue that the Hermit in HHB is a magician outside of direct association to Aslan. However, it seems quite clear that he is a servant of Aslan, and is under the rule of Aslan. It is also worth noting that he never uses magic for selfish needs, but only for others. This fits clearly with what 'good magic' is and with the character of Aslan.

57. Some might argue that the existence of the wardrobe and the magic tree in MN are examples of good magic in our world. While they are clearly good magic, they are only so because they are of Narnian origin. There is no such thing as good magic of our world, according the Narnia series.

58. *Collected Letters of C. S. Lewis*, pages 841-842.

59. *Harry Potter, Narnia, and Lord of the Rings*, page 144.

60. For much of Lewis's writings, this is a major theme. Most of his Christian life was an attempt to bring people back to the wonder of the supernatural, and to re-awaken the heart longings for "other worlds," such as Heaven. This can be most clearly seen, among other places, in his sermon "The Weight of Glory." Lewis also wrote two books on this subject: *The Abolition of Man* and

Miracles.

61. Paul Ford, *in* Jeffrey Shultz and John West, *The C. S. Lewis Encyclopedia* (Grand Rapids, MI: ZondervanPublishingHouse, 1998), page 121.

62. Christin Ditchfield, *A Family Guide to Narnia: Biblical Truths in C. S. Lewis's The Chronicles of Narnia* (Wheaton, IL: Crossway Books, 2003), page 58.

63. *Perelandra* (1943).

64. *The Great Divorce* (1946).

65. Randy Alcorn, *If God is Good...* (Colorado Springs, CO: Multnomah Publishers, 2009), page 209.

66. C. S. Lewis, *Letters to Malcolm: Chiefly on Prayer* (New York, NY: Harcourt, Brace & World, Inc., 1964), page 20.

67. In *The Complete C. S. Lewis Signature Classics.* (New York, NY: HarperOne Publishers, 2002), page 158.

68. Lewis, in a letter to Anne, dated March 5, 1961.

69. Marvin Hinten, *The Keys to the Chronicles: Unlocking the Symbols of C. S. Lewis's Narnia* (Nashville, TN: Broadman & Holman Publishes, 2005), pages 49-50

70. Ditchfield, *A Family Guide to Narnia,* page 75.

71. In all of his fiction, Lewis would try and point his reader back to solid morals and the Bible as much as possible, but without trying to preach at them. In this way he was able to cause more people to open their minds about Christianity. A good example would be his space trilogy. His concern for the salvation of others can also be clearly seen in his short novel, *The Great Divorce.*

72. Lewis, in his letter to Anne, March 5, 1961.

73. Most notable would be his popular *Mere Christianity* and the *Problem of Pain.* These were intended for the skeptics of Christian beliefs, with the hope of reinforcing the faith of believers and challenging skeptics of Christianity.

74. Some people have made the claim that this implies racism on the part of Lewis, who made the 'good guys' white, from England, and the 'bad guys' dark skinned, like the Middle Eastern peoples. This is an invalid argument for various reasons; see the next chapter.

75. This topic could easily take a small book to cover, but is outside the scope of this study. See Jerry Bergman, "C. S. Lewis: Creationist and Anti-evolutionist," *Journal of Creation,* vol. 23, num. 3 (2009), pages 110-115.

76. This belief of Lewis is covered in much more detail in chapter one of this book.

77. The British equivalent of the Newberry Medal Award.

78. Lewis, in his letter to Anne, March 5, 1961.

79. People often point to this and claim that Lewis was teaching astrology. This argument is discussed, and found wanting, in the next chapter.

80. Skeptics like to point out that the sacrifice of Aslan in LWW could not possibly be compared to Jesus' death on the Cross because Aslan died for just one human: Edmund. This passage in LB clearly shows this idea to be false.

81. Hinten, *The Keys to the Chronicles: Unlocking the Symbols of C. S. Lewis's*

Narnia, page 89.

82. This is most clearly seen in his short novel, *The Great Divorce*, his novel *Perelandra* and *The Last Battle*, and in numerous places throughout his theological writings.

83. An extraordinary book that discusses this in detail is Randy Alcorn's *Heaven* (Wheaton, IL: Tyndale House Publishers, 2004). It uses many of the concepts in LB as a foundation.

84. Paul Ford, *Companion to Narnia*, fifth edition (New York, NY: HarperSanFrancisco, 2005), page 363.

85. John Bunyan, *The Pilgrim's Progress* (New York, NY: Collier and Son Corporation, 1937 [originally published in 1678]), page 135.

86. Lewis, quoted in Heather and David Kopp, *Roar! A Christian Family Guide to the Chronicles of Narnia* (Sisters, OR: Multnomah Publishers, 2005), page 369.

87. Tom Peterkin, "C.S. Lewis, Chronicles of Narnia author, honoured in Poets' corner." *The Telegraph* (London, England). November 22, 2012. Retrieved from http://www.telegraph.co.uk/news/uknews/9694561/CS-Lewis-Chronicles-of-Narnia-author-honoured-in-Poets-corner.html.

88. An excellent resource on this topic is the forward to *Companion to Narnia* by Madeleine L'Engle, pages xv-xix.

89. Josh McDowell, *A Ready Defense* (Nashville, TN: Thomas Nelson, 1993), pages 381-385. See also, E. Hindson, and E. Caner, editors, *The Popular Encyclopedia of Apologetics* (Eugene, OR: Harvest House Publishers, 2008), pages 77-80.

90. Interestingly, some religious groups, such as the Mormons, do not believe it is good spiritually to drink even coffee, because they say the caffeine can be addictive. This is basically the same reason the Bible gives for not drinking 'strong drinks.'

91. In *The Complete C. S. Lewis Signature Classics*, pages 71-72.

92. Laurie Winslow Sargent and David Kopp, "Mercy! How the Wine Doth Flow in Narnia!" in *Roar!*, page 363.

93. The Jinn play a large role in Islamic mythology, where they can influence people for both good and evil. They are mentioned numerous times throughout the *Qur'an*, the holy book of the Muslims. See Sura 6:100; Sura 46:29-32; and Sura 72:1-15.

94. Lewis seems to have gotten the idea from George Macdonald, who wrote the book *Lilith* in 1895. Lewis is known to have greatly enjoyed this book and read it many times throughout his life.

95. In *The Complete C. S. Lewis Signature Classics*, page 701.

Printed in Great Britain
by Amazon